Sep 20

FIRST,
CATCH

FIRST, CATCH

Study of a Spring Meal

THOM EAGLE

Illustrations by Aurelia Lange

Grove Press
New York

Originally published in 2018 by Quadrille, an imprint of Hardie Grant
Publishing.

Published simultaneously in Canada
Printed in the United States of America

First Grove Atlantic edition: March 2020

ISBN 978-0-8021-4822-3
eISBN 978-0-8021-4823-0

Library of Congress Cataloging-in-Publication data is available for this title.

Grove Press
an imprint of Grove Atlantic
154 West 14th Street
New York, NY 10011

Distributed by Publishers Group West

groveatlantic.com

20 21 22 23 10 9 8 7 6 5 4 3 2 1

To my parents; and to Lola, of course

CONTENTS

MENU

Bread and pickles

Cured ~~Lamb fillet~~ sea trout, radish salad

(grilled?) Mackerel and tomatoes, alexander's green sauce

Salted potatoes, Lovage (?) butter

Sprouting broccoli + anchovy dressing

Sweet and sour celery (celery caponata?)

Rabbit Ragu

~~blood pudding~~ Sanguinaccio dolce

cheese

PREAMBLE

I spend a great deal of my time in the physical or imagined presence
of food. I wouldn't say that I was a greedy child, but it is a fact that
I once put so much chocolate in my mouth that I couldn't breathe.
People like to point out that all of my childhood memories – and
indeed many of my adult ones, too – are connected in some way
with what I was eating at the time. A teacake saturated with butter
in Great Aunt Dorothy's kitchen; hot waffles on a rainy promenade
in Belgium; Coca-Cola and vanilla ice-cream on a sunny Yorkshire
lawn with a border collie. On my third birthday I sat in the garden,
unwrapping toffees, my clumsy fingers dropping them one after
another into the newly dug sandpit. Although I don't think my
palate or nose particularly refined, they are certainly hard-wired to
my memory; my spots of time are almost all edible.

I suppose it's easy, looking back, to pick any narrative you like
from the hurried confusion of events that constitute a life, to find
inspirations, hints and foreshadowings. When I finished university,
sick of writing and of words and wanting most of all to work with my
hands, I turned towards the professional kitchen. My mother likes to
remind me, as if the progression had been inexorable, how at the age

of eight I expressed a wish to cook an entire roast chicken dinner and was duly guided through her carefully planned timetable for doing so in our little galley kitchen: when to parboil, when to pre-heat, when to remove and to keep warm and to strain was all noted down in a tight schedule. I had, as I cooked, the perhaps not entirely unjustified sense that a single misstep could bring the delicate waltz to a grinding halt; behind it, though, I heard the hiss of frozen peas meeting boiling water, the forceful shuffle of half-cooked potatoes, and all the other music of the kitchen which now fills my ears.

I had made cakes and jam tarts and so on before this, but that precocious chicken gave me the sense that, unlike baking, with its careful but apparently arbitrary proportions of everyday ingredients transformed in the dark, their rise or fall determined by the whim of the oven, cooking was not simply magic; if you paid attention it seemed you could make food do what you wanted it to do. It also, for that matter, showed me that not even the most meticulous of recipes is infallible, as the chicken came out rather pinker than it should, and so dinner was late in the end. Still, when I cooked a Christmas dinner for the first time last year in an equally restricted space, I found myself working to a similar timetable – the difference being, after years of cooking professionally, that the process was entirely in my head and in the rhythm of my arms. Aside from the paperwork, being a chef is mainly about juggling, with the food itself often something that emerges almost incidentally from a complicated interplay of pans, plates and people. It is very different – festive dinners aside – from cooking peacefully at home, where each thread of a meal can be joined easily to the next, or set aside to be picked up again at your leisure.

*

Even food I have never seen possesses me. I have a stronger mental picture of the picnic in *The Wind in the Willows* than of many of the real events in my own life. Whenever I travel, my appetite roams ahead, fuelled by ranks of essays and stories and memoirs, and sometimes by recipes. I seek out and devour food writing in all of its forms – from lengthy and flowery introductions, through drily academic histories to the tersely scribbled instructions you sometimes find tucked into old cookbooks. But when I think of all the recipes I have read, professionally or otherwise, stacked up as it were in one gigantic pile on an overflowing workbench, the main sensation I feel is frustration. All those neat little lists – take this, take that – as if cooking begins when you pick up an onion, or finishes as the dish goes on to the plate. So much more surrounds a meal and its making than just the bare facts of its enumerated parts. At the top of the page it just says 'two onions, chopped', but someone had to grow them, to pick them, to store and transport and buy them, all before you take them from the vegetable rack or the fridge, halve them from root to tuft, and peel off the outermost layers of brown parchment; before you cut first in a wedging arch and then across, remembering the cook who taught you to let the onion fall into its own layers rather than force it apart into rigid dice, and wondering perhaps in passing why you are doing so, when the other recipe said sliced, when the other recipe contained no onion at all. The Koreans have a description for the specific qualities of a person's cooking which translates as something like 'the taste of your hands'; they know, I suppose, that knowledge rests in muscle and bone, which is never written down.

I have nothing against recipes. In fact I use them all the time, and am suspicious of cooks who claim never to do so. Recipes are a record of social and emotional histories as well as a means of travelling to almost any country or place you care to name, including, of course, the past. Anyone who tries to separate food from all of these things cooks for reasons I do not understand; it can only, I think, be vanity, trading the deep satisfaction of time for immediate gratification.

Yet, while useful to cook from, there is so much that recipes miss. The satisfaction of peeling a ripe, thick-skinned tomato, for instance, or unzipping a pod of broad beans; the smell of rosemary hitting gently warming olive oil; the yielding of a wing of skate to a gently pressing finger; the sight of a simply laid table in spring, awaiting the arrival of both people and lunch. None of this can be captured in a written recipe. These are sensations we feel behind the lines of our cookbooks, but the rigid lists that now fill them leave little room in which to do so, let alone to think about what we will do with this dish once we have cooked it. 'Serve immediately', these instructions end, but who to? Even a thousand recipes don't make a meal.

Of all the contexts surrounding the acquisition and transformation of food, I think the meal itself is the most often forgotten. We cook in competition with ourselves now, imagining some bespectacled judge pacing around our chopping board and offering disparaging comments on our knife skills, our plating and our personal hygiene, while we collect and compare recipes of so-called genius and perfection, to be followed to the last detail. Whatever tortured dish emerges from such a process is designed not to be dug into with a questing fork, but to sit as it were under glass, to be admired one-on-one, alone. A plate is one part of a course, which is one part of a meal, so why fuss over the recipe so? I'd rather have, for example, a litre of wine, a pile of fresh pea pods, and many hands to peel and pour – with maybe a piece of cheese for afterwards.

It was after such a meal, the details of which I cannot remember exactly but which centred around a yearling sheep that we rubbed in oil and spice and buried whole in hot ash – or rather, it was after the resulting hangover had lifted – that I first began to compose and to compile the few notes from my own experience that follow. They do not, I should say, constitute a recipe book; with the meal in mind, they are arranged more in the order of the eating than of the cooking, and thus are about as far from that roast chicken timetable as they can be, except that they also sit at home, in a perhaps too-small kitchen, with family or friends on their way over, or pouring their first drinks. Some of my favourite cookbooks are those I know I will never use, but if you insist that food writing should be practical and try to cook from this book, I ask at least that you read it all the way to the end, to avoid any surprises – as of course you should with all recipes. In any case, I put these notes together not as a practical guide but to remind myself, as much as anyone, of all that comes out of a meal as well as all that goes into it – or, to put it another way, to demonstrate to my own satisfaction that there is so much more to food than just the cooking of it. At the very least I wanted to make some small contribution to the ongoing conversation we call cooking, which began when a deer or rabbit first fell into the fire, and will continue, perhaps, until the sun sinks under the western ocean for the final time.

1

ON CURING
WITH SALT

The thing to do is just begin; the question, of course, is where. We think of recipes as more-or-less scientific sets of instructions, little closed systems that start with an onion and finish 'at once', when in fact they are more like short stories – about history, about politics and about love, with obscure morals – told in a curious imperative. Every order given, to dice this or simmer that, has within it a memory – I diced this so that we could eat together; I simmered that to keep away the cold.

That's not always relevant, though, is it? Sometimes you just need to know the immediate facts. The fact is that there was an onion, chopped, and maybe some garlic; just a little, you understand. Anyone who's ever sat down to write a recipe knows how arbitrary the facts can be. A clove of garlic? One can be the size of four, or eight, or twenty smaller cloves – and then there's the strength. The more precise a recipe, the less accurate it gets; up to a point, anyway. There's no accounting for taste. Although a recipe presents itself and is experienced as a formula, a movement from idea and ingredient to an edible meal, it really is just a description of what was done, recipes are written backwards. When one says 'cook for ten minutes', it means 'I cooked it until it was cooked, and although this differs with the size, shape and construction of your pan, the fineness of your chopping and the particular make-up of your ingredients, I will say ten minutes'; recipes are lies, if generally useful ones. Behind each recipe as presented on the cookbook page, there is another recipe, told in actions rather than ingredients, working busily away, stirring and seasoning and checking; this recipe acknowledges that it could have become anything, that its beautifully plated and styled end result is not the only – or even the most desirable – assembly of its raw materials. It's just what the ingredients wanted to become this time – they could, really, have been anything. A recipe is a work in progress, one outcome of a long, silent conversation between cook and cooked, which started before anyone alive today thought to pick up a knife. It is a sleight of hand, focusing attention on the ingredients in a recipe, and not the process that puts them together. We are given twists and reinventions, exotic spices and forgotten cuts, all of which emphasize the things that make each recipe different, when we should be learning the things that make them the same. There is only one recipe, really: prepare your ingredients and cook them until done. Everything else is just a variation on that.

Where, then, to begin? What is the first thing you do when attempting a recipe? Check you have the main ingredients, I suppose. Very sensible. But the first thing you should really do is check you have enough salt.

If I could give one piece of advice to apprentice cooks it would be not to fear salt. Yes, too much can be bad for you; yes, some people should avoid it; yes, it is what makes the Dead Sea dead, but overall salt has done more good for humanity than harm. Seasoning, if anything, separates us from other beasts, changing feed to food and letting us take a deep and lasting pleasure in the business of fuelling our gross cells. Let's be clear – any recipe that contains only a 'pinch' of salt, or enough to 'correct' the seasoning at the end, is not to be trusted. The writer either does not like or does not understand food, or, if they do, is lying to you – more than usual, I mean. Salt should be added, sometimes with abandon, sometimes judiciously, at three distinct stages of cooking: helpfully, at the beginning, the middle and the end. Your average recipe only admits the last, which is the most subjective, a matter literally of taste; the first two affect the texture, the cooking and the basic physical make-up of your dish.

The first especially reaches back into history, the start of the story of any meal. I don't know if many people have looked at or visited old salt-pans; it is something I go out of my way to do. They are on eerie shores, unexpectedly desolate stretches of holiday coastlines – Kent, North Norfolk, St Monans, Sicily – in places where there is no beach, no cliff to speak of, just land which spills gently down into the water and up into the blankly blinding light, making it difficult, whether the day is overcast or bright, to distinguish one from the other. Where grounded boats seem to mushroom spontaneously amidst miles of dry land, and perfectly good footpaths end suddenly in water; where caravan parks huddle behind the sea wall, enjoying inward views of endless salt marshes while the waves crash out of sight between grey and grey. These are places where people used to fish, used to live and work, coaxing the sea into networks of channels and flat pools, sun- or fire-heated basins in which to rake and dry those crystals, tiny ziggurats of life. There are better ways of getting salt now, I suppose, but the salt-pans are still there – reminders that what we grab or grind in handfuls and sprinkles and pinches was once dragged bodily from the sea.

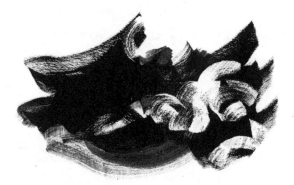

It is difficult now, with freezing and refrigeration and canning, with animals slaughtered every month of the year, with fresh food shipped in from other climates and much-lengthened growing seasons in our own, to appreciate the importance of salt throughout our history. We live in a world where everything is available, all of the time, where preservation has become a matter of taste and life-style, yet it was once a matter of survival. Everything that was not eaten almost as soon as it was picked, plucked or otherwise killed needed some intervention to make it last, to keep it from the long deaths of heat and time, and as often as not, this intervention came in the form of salt.

If you didn't have enough to salt down your hams and your sausages, to corn your beef, to preserve the catch of herring or cod, to pack in with enough beans and cabbage to last through the dark winter, then you would probably starve. Without the twin aids of refrigeration and sterilization, this meant a lot of salt. I've gone through kilos at a time just to make enough salt hake, ham or pickles to last a few weeks at a small restaurant in abundant Suffolk; I can hardly imagine the amounts that would have been needed in large households only a couple of centuries ago – heaps and heaps and heaps of it, and all raked out of the brine in odd little villages called Seasalter or Salthouse, Maldon or Trapani.

There is a curiously persistent belief that the former prevalence of spices in European cookery (a fashion that lasted well into the Georgian period) was simply a trick to mask rotting or at least past-its-best meat, an idea that is compelling but entirely untrue. For one thing, spices were very expensive, and used to further enrich only the very best dishes; for another thing, meat would not have been left to rot. If anything, the rich would have enjoyed their meat unhung and therefore much fresher than we would now find palatable, with chickens and small birds, even sheep and pigs, killed to order for the table – the lakes and hunting grounds attached to castles and stately homes were as much for convenience as for sport. The poor, on the other hand, would have eaten almost every-thing cured. A (or the) reason that offal formed such a large part of so-called peasant cuisines the world over is not because it was cheap, but because it was prized; as it wasn't well suited to curing, it was the only fresh meat that many people ever ate. Everything else was salted, smoked, dried or hung.

Some places at the edge of the world do largely without salt for their curing needs, and their food is peculiar to say the least. I know of the wind-dried fish and fermented lamb of the Faroe

Islands and Iceland only by reputation – which is fearsome – but the interest they arouse demonstrates their strangeness; their methods and flavours so alien that they beguile as much as they disgust. If modern cooks are often scared of salt, we are worried, when ageing or curing, by the lack of it – as we generally should be. The northern islanders made do without salt only because they had to. To dry it out of the sea, you need either long, hot days or plenty of firewood; in the absence of both, they let the air brine their food. For most other peoples throughout history, salting has been the first step in the often long processing of raw materials into edibility, and the most reliable way of laying stocks against the future's cold.

Of course there have been cellars, caves, icehouses, larders and so on for much longer than there have been refrigerators. Henry VIII's palace at Hampton Court has a corridor attached to the kitchen, so built – north-facing and with high stone walls – that the temperature still remains steady, around five degrees centigrade, as it has done for centuries. In the main, though, these storerooms would not have been capable of the long-term storage of food in an unprocessed state; the idea that everything should be available to us fresh and ripe at all times is a very recent one. A cellar might be cool, but the food put into it would have been dried already.

As with so many things, what was once a matter of absolute necessity has become a luxury; what was once in the hands of any housewife has receded into the professional world, made on the one hand in shining, sinister factories, and on the other artisanally and at greater expense. We still salt these days, but not to live. A fine air-dried ham, in the mountain style of Spain or Italy, is no longer simply a way to store enough protein to survive, but rather a cultural as well as culinary object, a store of peasant authenticity, cosmopolitan luxury and intense flavour. Maybe it is a sign that art for art's sake, or at least pleasure for pleasure's sake, still exists in a world that seems increasingly drained of the light of ritual and culture; or maybe it is just a sign that the manufacturers of *Jamón Ibérico* have worked out the cost of salt and the loss of time and weight against the price they can charge for a well-aged leg, and done the maths. Either way, at least there is ham, thin slices of it, to eat at a warm room temperature with too-cold beer.

I suppose making whole-muscle, bone-in charcuterie is a lot to ask of the home cook these days. Apart from the time and the storage space – few people have a room or corridor that is constantly cool and airy – you do need a lot of salt, kilograms of the stuff, certainly pure and preferably coarse, which does work out as quite expensive, even before you start worrying about the cost of the meat. If something goes wrong, as it sometimes does, then you have wasted not just a large portion of a possibly noble animal, but also large amounts of your own money. And there's certainly no shame in buying good things from competent professionals. Still, if you find yourself with the hind leg of an animal – not necessarily a pig – and you have no pressing need to eat it straight away, there are worse things to do with your time than to cure it.

I have twice made an air-dried mountain ham with hogget leg – the gamey meat of the year-old sheep, which matures into something really quite remarkable and pungent; at the moment I have three goat legs hanging in the rafters, and I can only imagine how they will taste. Northern Italians call such small hams 'goat violins' because of the shape and the way they are held for slicing, which is, if anything, another reason to make them. The loss of a hogget leg to rot notwithstanding, they were really quite simple to make and (perhaps more importantly) made all other curing seem easy. Once you have waited six months for a ham to dry into edibility, the salt and the air conspiring to replicate something like cooking on the raw flesh, a couple of weeks in the fridge seems like nothing. You have learned something that everybody used to know anyway – to put your faith in time and in salt. Watching the muscle and the fat slowly change during a longer cure is interesting, but it is just that – slow. Unless you obsessively check and squeeze it every day, the pace can be too subtle to really notice, like the hour hand slowly pushing the time away. This is where a quick cure can be useful. Such a cure, it should also be said, makes the ideal start to a simple spring meal.

For some reason, this is something that people tend to do mainly to fish, especially salmon – I suppose such a luxurious thing as gravlax, like a well-aged prosciutto, is fun to make yourself. You can make it with salmon if you like (I do), although sea trout is nicer when you can get it, but I also make it with lamb. The process is the point, really; once you have made the cure the other ingredients are secondary, except for the fact that you are going to eat them. Best to stick to something you like. I like curing lamb because it is so rarely seen, in this country at least; I like to imagine the mutton hams of Snowdonia and the Welsh Marches, the prized blackface loins and the peppered hogget shoulders of Romney Marsh, that we might have if only this country had embraced dry-curing – but that's beside the point. A quick cure like this, a matter of one or two nights in the fridge, is relatively stress-free, but if you lack time or space you can leave it out at a cool room temperature – the salt takes care of any danger.

So, say you have a couple of neat lamb loin fillets (though they could equally be skinned sides of trout): mix together coarse salt and granulated sugar, in an approximate ratio of six to four, and that's it, there's your cure. Make a layer of it in an appropriate container – deep enough to hold the fillets twice over, and made of something other than metal – pat your lamb dry, place it on the cure, then cover with the rest of the mixture, patting it over and round. You can flavour the cure if you want, with lemon or orange zest, fennel seeds, paprika, fenugreek, sumac, chilli, pepper or juniper – anything really. Spices are little details in a story, and here we are looking at the plot, as represented by 600 grams of coarse sea salt and 400 grams of granulated sugar. Granulated sugar is cheaper than caster sugar, but you can use the latter instead if that's what you have. Demerara could add its own particular flavour, but soft browns, light or dark, would quickly melt away in the juices expressed by your curing meat as it sits overnight at the bottom of your fridge. The salt and the sugar might melt anyway, depending on the exact temperature of your fridge or larder, the age of the animal and how long it was dead; this being the case, give the meat a poke and if it is softer than you would like, still as soft as raw meat, then make up another batch of cure, perhaps half as much this time, and re-coat the fillets.

The next day your lamb should be just-so, and will want rinsing and towelling dry, and perhaps to be left uncovered in the fridge to dry further. The slightly tacky layer that develops on a piece of cured animal protein, which might allow smoke to stick to its surface or, left long enough, further develop into a rich bloom of thick white mould, is called a pellicle. It is the tangible sign, alongside the pinkish swill in the bottom of your curing tub, of the moisture that has left your pieces of lamb, or indeed your sides of fish, a proof that your homespun cure has worked. If you are inclined to scepticism, cut into it, in thin slices, and as you lay them across a plain white plate, look at the depth of the colour, a version in oils of the now rather drab-seeming original meat. I like to partner this richness with raw vegetables, newly shaved or straight from the plant, which have themselves been subjected to the fresh violence of lemon juice and salt – enough lemon to make you wince, then enough salt to tame it. Salt, among its many virtues, tempers sourness and lets you taste the sweet within it, which may well be a metaphor for something but is certainly useful to know as you dress tiny broad beans, ivory ribbons of turnip or little slivers of violet artichoke and eat the lot with many hands around the table, much, much quicker than it was made… But we're getting ahead of ourselves. Your lamb or your fish will keep happily in the fridge while the rest of the meal emerges.

2

ON BOILING
AND PICKLING
WITH WATER

When I was an apprentice, washing dishes, peeling potatoes, whipping cheesecake mixes and otherwise making myself useful in the fairly nondescript kitchen of a small hotel, the sous-chef told me something that I've always remembered, possibly because it was one of the few things he said that wasn't obscene. The French, he said, have no less than seventeen different words for boiling water; or rather, like the Inuit and their snow, they have seventeen words to differentiate minutely between the several stages that lie between flat calm and a rolling boil. Water can be so many things, and the words we use affect the realities of what we do with it. These qualities are within the water; cooking simply makes them apparent. In the absence of seventeen distinct words for boiling water, we have to make the ones we have work a little harder.

Reading old cookbooks can be a fascinating, intriguing, occasionally frustrating and even disgusting hobby, but the books are often merely baffling, especially those from the Victorian era and thereabouts, when interested and scientific men started to intrude into a sphere that had always been the preserve of mere lifelong professionals and domestic experts. Efficiency and so-called 'nutrition' became key, often flying in the face of all evidence. It was observed that water at a full rolling boil was no hotter than water at a mere simmer, and that – despite what the French thought – there must therefore be no difference between the two in terms of efficacy of cooking; in order to save fuel, everything should be simmered. What we know now, and what anyone might in fact have observed had they utilized physical evidence rather than first principles, is that not only the heat but the motion of the water itself affects the cooking time; the rapid transfer of a rolling boil is what keeps green vegetables fresh and green, pasta *al dente*, and so on. With their insistence on simmering, these old cookbooks ask, essentially, that everything be stewed, which is why they demand a half-hour cooking time for sprouts or broad beans, and why, presumably, vegetables were not much loved at this time.

Whether because of this sous–chef's piece of wisdom or my own tendency towards daydreaming, I have spent a lot of time watching pots at various stages of boiling, and believe you can learn more from doing so than from almost any other activity, or at least any requiring an equivalent lack of physical effort.

Having first (of course) asked the bill–payer's permission, put a large pan of water over a medium heat, and wait. See if you can distinguish seventeen distinct stages of boiling – I'm not sure I can. Watch the first tiny bubbles rise from the bottom of the pan, as around a plump chicken cooking gently away; see how they group together in little spirals and whorls, into which you might drop a fresh egg to poach. A few minutes later, with the pan shimmering all over, whole unshelled eggs could slip in, on their way to coddling; next, the steady, gentle roil of boiling beetroot or carrots or potatoes, and so into the violence required for properly cooked broccoli or pasta, the sort of boil that needs sauces, dressings, colanders or ice baths arranged before you even begin. That's only five, but I'm sure a more observant cook than me could think of another twelve.

If you expand the remit to other boiling liquids there would be certainly more to be seen. Water, after all, is too thin to be of very much interest, and it boils away before it gets too hot. There is something very satisfying, however, about watching a tin of tomatoes turn from solid-in-liquid to one thicker substance, with the rising bubbles becoming wider and thicker as it does so, or seeing a pot of béchamel or polenta on the cusp between boiling liquid and angry paste, the whole surface roiling with steam, occasionally erupting in a lava-like blip. You could, if you paid enough attention, cook caramels and jams by eye alone, the development of sugar or pectin apparent in the thickening and stretching liquid, the sudden rises and falls, the sheen of heat over the surface of the pan... As these things are as much (or more) sugar as they are water, though, I'm not sure this is entirely relevant.

Water is often treated as a base level or reference point for culinary ability. When we say that someone can burn water, we are joking, but about something serious; when we say they can't even boil an egg, it is their ability to boil that is at question – the egg is a sideshow to the main event, just an excuse for hot water. I guess water is a fitting place to begin to learn how to cook – it's re-usable, for one thing, and of course it doesn't burn. More than that, though, we know that water is the beginning of things. Even the

Judaeo-Christian God, once he had turned on the lights, started off with water, and set his breath moving across it; our ancestors started out somewhere in the depths of old oceans, and so we know that life arises out of good salt water. You don't even need to cook it.

My kitchen is full of life. Better than that, it is thriving. Under the sinks, in a space just high enough for the airlocks, there are demi-johns of bubbling apple juice; on a high warm shelf there are jars of carrots, crab apples, peppers and turnips, each brined with its particular citrus and spice, and murkier pots of stalk and trim, ageing into edibility. A bowl of plain water and strong flour teems with fungus and bacteria. Today it smells good and sour, reminiscent of rye and pickle and milk – tomorrow it might smell of yeast, of warmth and buns and baking. All of these things are tiny ecosystems. When you add salt-and-sugar water to vegetable matter, you are calling down creatures from out of the everywhere, in Elizabeth David's wonderful phrase; given the right environ-ment, the useful ones – the *lacto-* or *aceto-bacillus*, the multitudinous yeasts – will come first, and they will protect their home from more dangerous interlopers. This, to me, is a magical thing. Pickle a few vegetables, and you are suddenly part of a wider world. You are living in symbiosis with ancient, invisible creatures, which, going about their own lives, almost incidentally create delicious things for you to eat. Most people, even if they had the inclination, don't have the space or time for beekeeping or smallholding; I would love to own a little pig, but instead I have jars of pickles, each one a self-contained culture, a wild community of thousands. Water and salt – to restate the point – give life, without the intervention of hand or heat.

It is the 'right environment' that is the key. Today we know the chemistry and the microbiology of what we are doing, or at least we know that it is known. I can only imagine the decades of trial and error, the centuries of co-evolution between bacteria and cooking technique that went into the development of gherkins, of sauerkraut and kimchi. Of course, if you have a microscope and know what you are looking for, you can check your pickles and your ferments for the right kind of invisible life; the point is that you don't really have to. All you have to do is create the correct conditions to set the process in motion.

Where cooks and householders were once fumbling in the dark, entrusting the year's crop of cabbages to what seemed like a magical transformation, an edible proof of invisible forces, today we can follow a map, and know that we are unlikely to lead anybody off its edge. Life likes water and it likes food, and bacteria are no exception; put one in the other and down they will come, and multiply quickly. Too quickly, in fact, and they will spoil both food and water, so we add salt, in significant but not enormous quantities, say around twenty grams to each litre of water, which is poisonous to most bacteria but not, crucially, to the *lactobacillus*. In its feeding it sours our brine, making it pleasantly tangy and inimical to pretty much any other form of life; packed tight and sealed against the air, with its potential cargo of moulds and yeasts, your ferment is both safe and complete.

Complete, but not finished. It is, after all, alive. As the salt water sours, the first group of bacteria are killed by the acid they themselves created, drowned in their own waste, and another lot arrive, stronger but still safe, 'friendly' in the current language surrounding the edible products of fermentation. The truth is, of course, that no bacteria or any other form of life, besides perhaps humanity, is friendly or unfriendly. If some of it is useful, in certain circumstances, it is only because we give it what it wants and make use of it, by allowing it to exist. Life just goes about its daily business with little concern for anything else, a fact we should be glad of; if any bacterium became capable of rational or at least malignant thought and took a dislike to our species, we would not have long left on the teeming, dying earth. Still, I suppose the word is 'useful', if only as a corrective to the rather unreasoning hatred of bacteria and other forms of microbial life which has taken root in recent decades. One reason fermentation feels so ancient and transgressive is that in almost every other area of cooking, and certainly within the professional kitchen, absolute hygiene is paramount – hygiene meaning the total destruction of other life.

To step away from the kitchen for a moment, look at antibiotics – a wonder-drug and a lifesaver to be sure, but also a blunt instrument which, used indiscriminately, destroys the useful and the ambivalent bacteria alongside the harmful ones. More worryingly, the routine use of these drugs in the meat industry, not even as medicine but to aid quick weight gain, has created strains of resistant pathogens of apparently comparable danger to AIDS and Ebola – and all because we are scared of microbes. To judge all bacteria by the harmful ones is like judging all cells by the virulence of cancer, or all animals by the destructive force of humanity. The routine use of antibiotics is like carpet bombing:

indiscriminate, destructive, and often doomed to failure.

It is the privilege of the healthy modern West to complain about the problems caused by our own advances. We should, of course, be glad that kitchens are cleaned regularly, that their stock is rotated and disposed of when unsafe, but still, the obsession with disinfecting, with washing or burning off any remnants of nature continues. I have read of people packing well-rinsed cabbage into sterilized jars, only to add a laboratory-grown bacterial culture; this seems, it must be said, like a waste of precious time. The point to remember is this: most things will naturally sour, cure or ferment, if only you let them. Just put the salted cabbage in the jar and let time do the rest. The mystique surrounding sourdough bread – some people's insistence on using starters months, years, generations old – only obscures the heart of the matter: that wheat, being covered in natural yeasts and bacteria, wants to grow sour. Much of the history of bread-baking in Britain, in fact, where culturally we seem to have had less tolerance for the products of wild fermentation, is the story of avoiding the formation of sourdough, which seemed to carry the physical taint of sin. Purge out the old leaven, Paul told the Corinthians, and be a fresh batch of dough, not yet bloated with corruption and time. If our baking ancestors had known of the teeming mass of airborne spirits that caused this sourness, then bread would probably have been banned altogether, the name of Baker become anathema in the land.

To put it another way, it is easier to make sourdough than it is not to, and the same is true of certain kinds of pickles. To not make pickles, you have to carefully wash and dry your vegetables, maybe trim and sort them; some need keeping in water with lemon in the fridge, some in paper bags at room temperature, some in the cool dark, some warm and dry – and having done this, they need using within a few days. Pickles, by comparison, are a slovenly affair. The less you can get away with washing and peeling them the better, really; you want the bacteria that clings to their skins. Any actual grit or mud needs removing, of course, but gently; rinse, don't scrub. After that it's merely a matter of cutting everything into roughly similar sizes, packing it into jars, and brining.

With such a simple process, you can afford to take care of the details. The most versatile brine, I find, is made with twenty grams of salt to each litre of water; in the world of fermentation, brines are measured by the weight of salt as a percentage of the water, so we are making a two per cent brine. In my experience such a weak brine does not need heating to dissolve the salt, which is easily done with vigorous stirring. Boiling does, on the other hand, serve to drive off the chlorine in tap water, which could otherwise inhibit the desired bacterial growth. Some people use bottled water for pickling, but that is something I really cannot bring myself to do, though you might feel otherwise. If you do, then stir away; if not, then let your boiled brine cool to at least a warm room temperature before pouring over the vegetables, or you will defeat your whole effort.

What vegetables, though? If you have small cucumbers, as they say, then make gherkins, in which case the addition of dill or fennel fronds and a couple of cloves of garlic is pretty much mandatory. Under-ripe tomatoes ferment very well, with a pleasing fizz, and so do ripe ones, for that matter; you can eat the former as a pickle, but the latter will collapse a little and have the potential to become a very good fish soup (with the addition of some fish, of course). We might return to this later. These aside – and unless you grow your own; small cucumbers and under-ripe tomatoes are quite hard to come by – I would recommend you make a mixed pickle, a fairly forgiving ferment. That doesn't mean it's a free-for-all, though, or at least only within certain parameters.

I always try, in my mixed pickles, to include at least one brassica, one allium and one citrus fruit. The citrus, normally halved lemons or heavy, thick-skinned oranges, is mainly there to sit on top and keep the vegetables below the brine. I could use a stone or those special fermenting weights, but in fact the flavour of the citrus helps keep the pickle balanced, with a fresh acidity that is quite different from the sour funk of the other vegetables. Brassicas and alliums are ubiquitous across the pickling world, of course, even in our own vinegar-led culture, and for very good reason: cabbage intensifies and onion mellows until the two meet in a wonderful sweet-and-sourness. I say cabbage and onion, but you could use most things from those families. Apart from the usual white, red and sweetheart cabbages, turnips, mustard greens and kale stalks ferment very well. The under-used kohlrabi, shaved into ribbons or cut into appley wedges, is excellent as part of a mixed pickle, but I would generally steer clear of cauliflower – it tends to make everything smell like old cauliflower. White onions, brown onions, red onions, spring onions, leeks and garlic all ferment very well in their various ways, as do wild garlic, chives, garlic chives, and everything else that sails under that particular banner. If you have a lot of wild garlic at the right point of the season, you can pickle the buds into a kind of pungent caper.

*

As I make rather a lot of these mixed pickles, I tend to colour code mine. Into one jar (or rather, one often-poorly-sealed plastic tub) goes the kohlrabi, white onion, standard white or pointed spring cabbage, sticks of celery, a few cloves of garlic and the occasional turnip, all sat beneath a lemon; into another, red cabbage, beetroot, radishes, carrot and red onion, under a couple of halved oranges. I could, to be honest, put almost anything in there, and it would come out stained a bright purple. For some reason, the pink pickle always seems to work better, though whether that is down to the combination of ingredients or because I think it looks nicer and tend to look after it more, I'm not sure. At any rate, the now-purple brine has a life beyond its pickled contents: apart from making an excellent pick-me-up, especially when enjoyed after a shot of raki, like a Turkish pickleback, it makes a very pleasing dye for boiled eggs when left to sit in it overnight.

These pickles, especially the white ones, go very well with cured meat or fish, as well as waking up the tastebuds and stomach like a good aperitif, and so we often have them with drinks or as a starter. Personally, though, I can eat them at almost any stage of the meal or indeed the day. To many, in fact, it is pickles that make a meal a meal. A bowl of rice porridge at the end of a back-breaking day is just a bowl of rice porridge, but the addition of some kimchi makes it dinner; just as a few handfuls of sauerkraut stewed with that desiccated piece of salt pork can help you see past the bitter winter to the first days of spring.

3

ON SEASONING
WITH WATER

All of this, and we haven't even started cooking yet — though I suppose that depends on what you mean by cooking. There was the water for the brine, heated just enough to dissolve the sugar and the salt, and to drive off some unwanted chlorine; I'm not sure that counts, though. Cooking, it seems to me, should be transformational, should surely involve a process that cannot be undone. It is not just heating up some water and letting it cool down again, or drying some beans only to rehydrate them, but an irreversible step away from the natural, perhaps towards the unknown — the French chemist Hervé This (pronounced Tiss) once 'unscrambled' eggs — depending on how familiar you are with what you are cooking.

In this school of thought, perhaps we *have* started cooking; the action of fermentation on raw vegetables is certainly not reversible and, for that matter, is very similar to the play of heat and water on their flesh and cells. If you let the process go too far, you can end up with a rather pungent mush, reminiscent of those Victorian stewed greens. Even before fermentation properly begins, say when you are rubbing coarse dry salt into shredded cabbage to make sauerkraut or perhaps a kimchi, you can see and feel the abrasive effect it is having on the vegetable, leaching out the juices and turning it that dense bright green. Some methods of curing fish and meat, too, for example the acidic bath we give to *ceviche, escabeche, scabeche, ceveach* or pickles such as rollmops, act upon the flesh in such a similar way to gentle heat – coagulating the protein, rendering the muscle opaque and fibrous – that it is referred to as 'cooking', though always with those quotation marks because, I suppose, we think that cooking involves heat.

Maybe this is an old-fashioned view, which merely reflects the fact that almost everything in the traditional British kitchen was cooked (by heating), or perhaps it is because there is the sense, deep in the meaning of the word, of boiling or burning. At any rate, the word has always also meant mulling over, preparing, combining, and whether it is cooking or pre-cooking, prep or even just mixing things together, it still needs doing, and it is often the hidden things that you do to ingredients far ahead of time that have the biggest effect on them.

Look at those pickles. Depending on how long you have allowed them to ferment (a week is normally quite enough, and they will happily live on in the fridge after that), though they look more or less like raw vegetables, floating in cloudy water, under the surface they have completely changed, flooded with foreign bodies, macerated in their acidic waste, fibrous and other-wise tough surfaces rendered crunchable and pleasant to eat. You would struggle to do so much to them with the crude application of heat.

There are lots of things you can do with fermented vegetables. Korean temple cuisine, for one, relies almost entirely on them as building blocks of flavour, as does, to a lesser extent, mainstream Korean food and indeed most of the food of South East Asia, of China and Japan. Ferments of pulses and rice, of seaweed and fish, alongside the more familiar pickled vegetables, combine into a flavour profile that is distinctly alien to that of Europe and even North Africa and the Middle East, with the ubiquitous warmth of onion replaced by the deeper savour of soy, the high tang of spring onion and vinegar – but for our pickles this initial ferment was the beginning and end of their journey. They are an excellent snack, and probably best enjoyed by themselves, or with bread and good cheesy butter; although they are really just seasoned vegetables, fermentation has made them assertive enough to hold their own – though I suppose a cocktail, a strong bitter one, wouldn't go amiss.

With our vegetables, the water and the salt were a means to an end, a way of trapping and holding those particularly useful bacteria while they did what we wanted them to do; the salt, remember, is just a way of keeping out the wrong sort of bacteria, though its seasoning properties are certainly appreciated. In other situations and with other ingredients, the brine itself is the whole point – a miraculous-seeming way of transferring salt into solid objects; I am talking about brining meat. This is another process that would once have mainly been done out of necessity and as a precursor to other methods of curing. Say you want to smoke some herring, as well you might; although smoked oily fish is, happily, delicious, smoking is really a way of preserving a highly perishable catch by drying out the flesh and at the same time bathing it in antimicrobial smoke. There is, presumably, no way that the fishwives of Yarmouth knew of microbes, but they must have known their process worked. Anyway, because herring, as well as mackerel, sardines and so on, will spoil in literally a matter of hours, you need to preserve them until the smoke gets to them – hence the brine.

It is the same for a leg or side of pork, which comes out of the cure as ham or bacon, ready, again, for the smoker. As meat and fish can go much more unpleasantly off than vegetables, the brine you use is stronger, often as high as twelve or fifteen per cent for traditional cures. Nowadays, though, as you will presumably be working in partnership with a refrigerator and don't require your meat to last you through the long months of winter, the cure is more in the region of six to ten per cent salt, depending on how long you intend to keep your meat in brine for.

I suppose the obvious question is why do we brine at all, with no need to preserve fresh meat? Why do we keep meat in salt water? Well, the first reason is the salt, and the second is the water. It's all to do with osmosis. As we all know, most things are mostly water, and certainly most things we eat are; those pickles are pretty much entirely water, especially if you used cucumber or celery. As I understand the matter, salt water cannot bear the sight of sweet water, and will breach cell walls, even the integrity of muscle and flesh, to mix with it and so average out the saltiness; it is possible a biologist would explain things slightly differently. Whatever the reason, if you put a piece of meat, even a very large one, in a salt-water solution, it will gradually become seasoned from the outside in, all the way to the bone if you leave it for long enough. Now, this isn't really necessary all of the time. When roasting, say, a good crackly pork joint or leg of lamb, the amount of salt required to dry and crisp the skin means that you don't really want it seasoned right through; if you find the sliced flesh bland, coarse salt sprinkled over it at the last minute seems to do the job better. Brined roast meat, especially fattier cuts, can acquire a kind of generic curedness, an almost clumsy exaggeration of flavours, which makes everything taste vaguely of sausages. When roasting in the traditional British sense, over high flames, you should be using meat of a quality that wants neither the heavy seasoning nor the curative qualities of brine.

Longer roasting requires greater intervention. Barbecued meat, for example – proper American barbecued meat, where briskets or shoulders or entire pigs are subjected to low smoky heat for half a day or more – benefits greatly from a salty bath. The long cooking process, much longer than almost anything else we call cooking, the acridity of the burnt outer bark and its casing of spice, would bulldoze the natural taste of the meat if it didn't have enough seasoning to stand up for itself. I've had barbecued, properly smoked, pulled pork shoulder that must have been days in the making – but they hadn't brined the damn thing, and so it tasted of nothing: tender, smoky nothing. You can, of course, add seasoning at the end of the process, when you chop or pull the meat and add your barbecue sauces, your vinegar and sugar and chilli, but the salt never seems to penetrate the dense fibres in the same way, and the amount you need to add is really quite alarming.

Similarly, any meat you intend to boil for a long time – hams, tongues, corned beef – demands a heavy brining. Salting the cooking water, as you do with pasta and vegetables, can only do so much, even in the hour or so a hock takes to become tender. The brining these cuts receive moves beyond seasoning and into the domain of curing, which is to say it begins an irreversible process which entirely changes the character of the meat, tenderizing as it tightens. Usually this involves saltpeter (potassium nitrate), a key component of gunpowder, as well as of hams and corned beef. Besides keeping such long-cured meats safe to eat, it penetrates right through the muscle and keeps them that blushing pink; you couldn't achieve that simply with the cooking water. In general, then, I brine meats to boil or to smoke, but leave grills and roasts alone. The exception to this rule is your roast turkey, and this is less to do with salt than, yes, water.

Like a lot of people, I have never really got along with turkey. It's not something we had for Christmas at home (a leg of pork, thank you), and when I did eat it, for festive school meals and so on, it wasn't shown at its best. Like all white meat, turkey tends towards dryness, and their enormous size doesn't help; nor does the fact that most people only cook them once a year. You don't get really good at cooking something – or doing anything, in fact – until you have done it over and over, and in a certain degree of calm. Then, after a few goes, you can try to do it quickly, while doing dozens of other things at the same time. You'll still probably mess it up, but you might have learned a few tricks along the way. I never had a turkey cooked well until I spent Thanksgiving in the United States, with a rather sprawling family in the depths of upstate New York; so sprawling that we had to eat the two turkeys, the green bean casserole, the mincemeat pies, the biscuits, and the mashed and sweet potatoes in shifts, children first, then the elderly, then the rest of us, by which point a fair amount of eggnog had been passed around. I particularly enjoyed the pies, and the creamy, roux-thickened gravy, but the turkey itself was the real surprise: a good surprise, juicy and tender and well-flavoured all the way through. It had been brined.

The effect of brining is not the same as simply soaking or injecting with water, as is done to bacon, ham and even scallops to cheaply pump up the weight; this additional liquid escapes on cooking, leaving the meat if anything drier than before. Brining, along with its seasoning properties, alters the structure of muscle cells in such a way that they are able to hold on to the moisture they contain, keeping your turkey plump and giving to the knife and the tooth. Now, in upstate New York in late November, you don't have to worry particularly about refrigeration. Assuming you have pans or tubs or bowls big enough, you can leave your turkey to brine in the backyard for a couple of days, and your chief worry will be larger wildlife than the microscopic. You have to be a little more careful in a temperate climate, where even over Christmas you can't guarantee the weather will stay cold enough to keep raw meat outside. In that case you could use a much stronger brine, a full old-fashioned curing brine, but that would really change the structure of your turkey – start to cook it, as it were, and maybe dry it out. And even if it didn't, you'd then have to soak it before you cooked it, and where would you do that? Best to steer clear of turkey altogether, to my mind. Even when they are very good, they aren't really that good, and if you aren't intending to feed three shifts' worth of people, they're probably too big; let's leave turkeys. I really only mentioned them to make a point, which is about salt and water.

Now, good chicken legs respond as well to brine as they do to slow cooking, but if you really want to observe the effect that brining can have on meat, get hold of some wild rabbit. Rabbit used to be one of the most popular meats in Britain – look through old cookbooks and you'll find dozens of recipes for it, in hashes and fricassees, casseroles and pies, roasts and stews and pasties. If it isn't now, I think it's mainly because people don't know how to cook it: it's dry, it's bony, it's stringy, it used to be called Peter and wear a little blue jacket... Some of these things are unchangeable, but others can be easily avoided by the judicious use of brine – about a five per cent brine, or perhaps a little stronger, in which case it'll need a thorough rinse and even a brief soak before you carry on cooking it. Unlike turkeys, even several rabbits – four, say, suitably jointed – will fit happily in most fridges when packed into a four-litre ice-cream tub, covered with cold brine and left overnight to quietly transform, but we'll get back to this. There is more to salt water than brine.

4

ON FISH AND
SALT WATER

A meal seems to be occurring. We have our pickles to snack on, and in that hypothetical brining rabbit, we have a possible main course, perhaps our dry-cured fillets of lamb or sea trout as a starter… I still haven't decided, though I suppose you may well have done. At any rate, that's a long way off; we're still talking about water, and nobody's done any cooking yet.

When I think about water, I often recall that when I was younger we had a beermat, acquired presumably by one of my older brothers from a pub, which bore on it the W.C. Fields quotation: 'I never drink water, fish **** in it'. It has never been clear to me which bodily function was originally indicated by that row of asterisks, but the remark does, its glamourization of alcoholism aside, make the interesting point that a substance we rely upon for life, that we associate with cleanliness (next to godliness, of course), with purity, baptism and rebirth, is in its natural state often filthy, salty, green or muddy, filled in every inch with life, some visible, some not, some capable of doing us deadly harm and some capable of becoming dinner. Everything comes from water, everything comes from the sea; stick your hand into it and you touch something living. Such is the world that fishermen cast their rods or their nets into, and it is no wonder, when you think about it, that fishing and fishermen are understood metaphorically across the world: that the Fisher King of the Grail legends was a fisher and not a huntsman or a kitchen porter; that the Christian disciples were made fishers of men; and that the Daoist sage Zhuangzi chooses the 'Joy of Fish' for his debate, and not that, say, of sparrows.

Despite, or perhaps because of all this, I took a long time to come around to fish-eating, and fish and the sea remain deeply mysterious, even a little terrifying to me – quite a lot, in fact. It is the way, I think, that it is all one thing; all of the oceans are inter-mingled. It might be unlikely that a colossal squid suddenly rears out of the water off Margate Sands, but it is not impossible; perhaps that is an angler fish nibbling at your toes... Although stories persist of creatures like the Yeti, Bigfoot and the Wendigo, we know really that such terrestrial cryptofauna cannot be real. There's no space for them, really; the world is mapped. In comparison, the seas seem to contain everything that has been in them since the darkness before time. If you can sail from Australia to the UK in one unbroken journey, it doesn't seem unlikely that something else could swim here from the late Jurassic, say. The oceans are vast abysses, and they are full, mostly, of monsters; when we imagine horrors, or the denizens of other worlds, we often give them the features of fish: tentacles, vast gaping mouths full of needle-thin teeth, gawping bug-eyes – these are the things that nightmares are made of. I suppose our association of the oceanic with the alien is hardly surprising when you consider that the water is in fact an alien environment, a crushing weightless place in which we cannot survive; though given the genesis of life at sea, it is really we who are the aliens, the mutants, filtering oxygen out of nothing as we indiscriminately drag up fish to suffocate on deck in the hot dry air – this is, at any rate, what I imagine octopuses and other of the more intelligent ocean-dwellers must think of us, if they think of us at all, as they go about their frankly mysterious business.

So on the one hand, life; on the other, darkness, terror and death. Fishing, in fact, must be one of the few truly dangerous professions left in the so-called developed world. Even with lifejackets, coastguards, radio, and every modern amenity for both avoiding and recovering from disaster, it is still deadly: nine-and-a-half British fishermen (on average) die every year as a result of accidents at sea. I don't think ten chefs or food journalists die each year from work-related injuries; bakers rarely fall into their ovens, and the good people of Blythburgh do not walk in terror of their ravenous pigs. There is a level of danger accepted in the getting of seafood which is unparalleled in the food industry, perhaps justified by a sort of knightly romance, a sense of quest and hunt, which is attached to the fishing industry. I once found it strange, reading *Moby-Dick*, that people would do something as dangerous as actually hunting whales through the sea, with lances and rowing boats and nets, simply to get lamp oil and perfumes. Commercial fishing is, at least, more useful than that; we eat the stuff, after all, and we're always being told to eat more of it. Eat better, would be more to the point.

Still, I don't intend to lecture you on sustainable fish consumption, on the importance of eating a variety of species, especially the ugly, the under-used, the more difficult to prepare and cook. For one thing, I hardly know anything about it. Fish stocks, obviously, are ever-changing things, and vary with the season and the weather, as well as with the depredations of humanity upon their habitats, their food sources and themselves. Keeping up with what is considered good or even okay to eat is a difficult task, and one I tend to leave to our fish supplier. A former fisherman himself, he deals chiefly with the dayboats going in and out of Lowestoft, the last remnants of the once-mighty fleet that animated the now rather run-down port, where the dilapidated Sea Breeze social club greets you as your train pulls in through the still-working harbour, on your way, generally, to somewhere else. The little town must once have truly been a sight to behold at the height of the herring season, when the women would travel from Yarmouth, Grimsby and Scotland to process the catch that the fishermen landed, scales and salt glinting in hair, nails, clothes, gutters and roofs, the streets covered with silver and fighting the stink of oily fish, the flesh of which does not last long out of the water.

The comparatively few boats that are left still bring in some herring – I have some pickling in the fridge right now, landed just the other day – but those vast bonny shoals have, if they still exist at all, gone elsewhere, and the boats must catch what they can and sell it, and to do that they need customers who will buy what there is, not come only for the premium flatfish, the loins of cod, the suspicious crevettes. More so than with any other ingredient, it is best with fish to let your shopping experience decide what you are having for dinner. Perhaps, as I did after reading an excellent Stephen Harris piece, in which the chef of The Sportsman created a feast using head, skirt, roe, bones and flesh of a large turbot, you might head to the fishmonger with your heart set on a fine big flatfish – but if it is not there on the slab, or worse, it is there but slack and grey-eyed, a day past its best, then frankly you will have to give up on your dream. Cook something else. Worse things, as they say, happen at sea.

The very fact that this needs stating, I think, shows the uneasiness with which people regard fish, and the sense we have that they are different, not just from us but from the other animals that we eat. In this, at least, we are not alone. It would seem that fish have always been regarded as something quite other than meat, from the ancient Athenians, who ate almost exclusively fish, keeping their land animals for the gods, to Catholic Europe, which, most notably in medieval times, set aside a great many days for fasting and for fish-eating. The implication is that all eating is more or less sinful, on a sliding scale down from cannibalism, through red meat, to fish and vegetation; we might remember that the eating of animals at all was a sop to the debased postdiluvian world, as

Jahweh realized that his creations would never quite be able to control themselves.

Anyone who has worked in a restaurant will have noticed that a lot of people, devoutly or not, still eat fish on Fridays (the chippy is usually heaving, too); abstention has become a treat. This is not, I think, how the rule would have been experienced originally, at least by the rich, monks and the priesthood, whose meals consisted not of a main protein and trimmings, but of a number of different dishes and delicacies: fish, fowl, fresh and salt meat, cakes, pastries and so on. The injunction to eat fish would, rather than involving a straight swap between creatures, have meant the loss of a great deal of variety at table – though I doubt anyone (I'm still talking about rich people) went hungry because of it. Even the most devout were still governed by the questionable taxonomy of the church elders, who at various points decided that beaver, goose, puffin, and even baby or foetal rabbits could be counted as fish. At any rate, although fish may now be eaten as a pleasurable rarity rather than under duress, the distinction between it on the one hand, and birds and mammals on the other, is still maintained. Many people, in my experience, who describe themselves as vegetarian are, in fact, pescatarian, and for them fish are not just biologically but morally other – outsiders to whom taboos do not apply.

Let's get back to cooking, which, with regards to fish, is something that seems to scare most people – almost as much as not cooking it. I would happily eat raw fish every day for the rest of my life, and it is my go-to meal when I feel I've been over-indulging on rich meat, cheese and alcohol, which is, I suppose, fairly often. The pleasure of good sushi is the absolute precision of its preparation: the sharp glint of the long knives, the soft cupping of rice and seaweed, all of which, unless you are willing to devote years of your life to mastering the craft, is best left to the professionals, I feel. If I crave sushi at home, I tend to just eat sticky rice and pickled ginger; if you let anyone who knows about sushi talk at you for a while, they'll tell you, probably several times, that it is all about the rice anyway.

Originally, of course, sushi was all about both rice and fish (as it still is), with the rice, inoculated with koji bacteria, being used as a medium to ferment the fish. Now, 'fermented fish' is a pair of words that most people do not wish to see together – especially in this country, with our rather puritanical attitude towards decay (remember the sourdough?); fermented vegetables are viewed with suspicion, so multiply that by the suspicion of those sea-dwelling aliens and you have a recipe for – well, come to think of it, you don't have a recipe for anything, at least not one that will be followed.

This, really, is an absurd prejudice. Think of Worcestershire sauce, probably one of the most delicious creations of humanity, a shot of sweet umami so good it can make cheese on toast taste even better; I have never met anyone who doesn't like it, and nor would I wish to. The recipe is secret, but we know it contains anchovies – fermented anchovies – the kind we buy in little tins. In this unadorned state they are rather more divisive, I suppose, but most adult palates would agree that, with the fishiness aged and fermented out of them, they attain a deep, pure flavour, impossible to get from any other source, at least in present-day Europe. Nampla and similar Asian fish condiments give a similar body to all manner of dishes, and they hark back to garum and to liquamen, the universal seasonings of ancient Rome, fermented anchovy sauces which filled the dockyards and the kitchens with their perva-sive hum. Mention garum to someone and they will probably react with either bafflement or disgust. How, they'll say (assuming they have any idea what you are talking about), how could the Romans, with their taste, their refinement, their reputation as gourmets, or at least gourmands, cover seemingly everything they ever ate with this wretched substance? The answer, of course, is that firstly, it isn't, and secondly, they didn't.

I have made garum myself – following methods culled from other cooks and from academic research into the vast industry that supplied the entire Empire with it – not, admittedly, from ancho-vies, but separately, as the Romans would in fact have done, from all sorts of gut and trim, squid, mackerel, and from the livers of monkfish. The Romans simply salted their fish and left them in the Mediterranean heat; coastal Suffolk has a rather more change-able climate, so I left mine in the plate-warmer at work for ten weeks, and I can tell you that the end result, when well aged and nicely filtered, is really very much like fish sauce, which is hardly surprising. The squid batch, to be fair, was densely black, but the mackerel – a fellow pelagic fish to the anchovy, so perhaps the closest to the classic version of the three that I made – ended up a deep translucent amber, salty and well flavoured, but subtle enough that I could use it as the main component of a dressing to accompany cod cheeks. A longer ageing process would, I think, yield a stronger sauce, more suited to use as a background seasoning, which is how the Romans would generally have used it. I have a book, Andrew Dalby's *The Classical Cookbook*, which attempts to turn ancient recipes into ones useable in the modern kitchen. The author notes that a Roman recipe, asking perhaps for a sauce of mustard, pepper, honey, garum, wine, coriander, asafoetida, vinegar and oil, sounds bizarre to the modern eater, yet the lost qualifier, of course, is the quantities. A sauce of mustard, salt, pepper, sugar, garlic, vinegar and oil could be inedible if you didn't know what you were doing; if you did, it could be a salad dressing. All things in proportion is the moral here, especially fermented fish.

Even if you are a fan of the modern Roman – or indeed the Neapolitan, Venetian or Sicilian – use of anchovy, in which the salted fish finds its way into extremely pungent dressings and melting pasta sauces, or on top of pizzas and hard-boiled eggs, there is still a leap to be made from the use of fermented fish as, essentially, a condiment, to eating it as the main event. As I've mentioned before, I have recently become fascinated by the cuisine of the Faroe Islands, built as it is around the thin and wavering line between fermentation and rot, where mutton is not considered ready until it sports a thick blue mould, and fish is left to age without the arresting power of salt. I say age, but you could equally say dry, mature, ripen or decay, as well as the more all-purpose term 'ferment'; the way we view food products of this kind is as much cultural as personal, and as much irrational as anything else, as disgust often is. Negative stereotypes of Chinese food, for example, have often focused on things such as thousand-year eggs, implying that the Chinese will happily eat something considered, in the Western mind, almost comically foul; meanwhile, much of Asia winces at our enthusiastic consumption of the festering corpse of milk – and everyone winces at the Faroe Islands. I have, at the moment, a number of small plaice hanging in the breeze, which I am attempting to age without saline intervention, though lacking the proper battering climate I kept the fish for a few days in a dehydrator before abandoning them to the elements. I must confess, I don't know what I'm going to do with them next. Cook them, I suppose.

5

ON COOKING
FISH IN WATER

The Italians, who perhaps more than any other Europeans seem to live out their lives through the medium of food, have a saying to the effect that, since fish dwell and thrive in water, they must be drowned in wine. The fact that, since fish dwell and thrive in water, they must really be drowned in air, and at any rate are best finished off with a sharp blow to the head, is rather by the bye, as the proverb is actually referring not to the killing but to the proper cooking of fish – specifically to poaching. Poaching, of course, is a variety of boiling which requires the gentlest of touches, especially when applied to fish. Every aspect, in fact, of the existence of a piece of fish, from its watery life to its decay and its cooking, happens at a colder level than that of most land animals.

As they have co-evolved to live, as it might be, in the depths of the North Sea, the bacteria that live on and inside fish go about their work at a lower temperature to our own. The microbes that enact the decay, for example, of a pork chop are rendered pretty much out of service below five degrees centigrade; this is not the case with fish, which is why it is kept on ice and why it will go off so quickly – and smell so badly – if kept for too long in a regular domestic fridge. It varies, of course, but the flesh of most fish is cooked, which is to say the muscle fibres start to separate from the bone and from each other, and the proteins coagulate into opacity, at around forty degrees, about ten degrees cooler than even rare steak. Subject a fillet or even a whole fish to hard boiling and it will quickly become dry, almost grainy to the tongue, and certainly unpalatable. It is a curious fact that, *sous-vide* and slow-roasting aside, we tend to use cooking mediums far hotter than we wish our food to be. As even gently bubbling water hovers around 100 degrees, recipes for using it to cook fish, in combination with various aromats − bay, lemon peel, fennel, garlic, and of course wine − tend to err on the side of caution in the application of heat.

In general, you will be asked to first boil the water with your chosen additions, to infuse their flavour into the liquid, which you then allow to cool; this sort-of herbal stock is known by its French name of *court-bouillon*, or short-broth. You then add your fish to the bouillon, return it to the boil, then remove it from the heat again, this time leaving the fish to cool with it. Fish (most often salmon) cooked in this way is − or rather was, this being a method that has fallen out of fashion − generally served cold, even in its jellified broth; as I said, people don't really do this any more. I did once attend a garden party where the plates of cold cuts were each garnished with an entire example of whatever animal or cut the meat was from; so the ham was illustrated by a whole bone-in glazed ham complete with white-cuffed leg, the chicken had a whole bird masked in béchamel and dotted with tomato roses, and the plate of salmon was topped with a whole poached fish, its naked pink flesh re-covered with neat scales of cucumber and moistened with aspic. As I gazed at it, someone handed me a Kir Royale and the picture was complete.

I can't say I have poached much fish in my life, professionally or otherwise, but there is something about the clear, direct flavour of it that I really enjoy. There is a Neapolitan preparation of sea bass that involves poaching it in 'crazy water', the craziness being provided by red chillies in the broth. This is a dish I first read about years ago, in Diana Henry's *Crazy Water, Pickled Lemons*, but only actually ate quite recently, in a rather knockabout trattoria in the Spanish Quarter of Naples itself; it was very good, if not perhaps quite as good as I'd imagined it being. We associate Mediterranean fish cookery more readily with extreme heat than with such gentle processes: the charcoal grill, the *plancha*, the smack of heat and salt air; we learnt these things from Rick Stein, from the better sort of gastropub, from holidays and TV, and at the same time we learnt to actually eat the fish we have. In place of the neat fillets of one or two white fish nestled in chip-shop paper and fine white china alike, came the whole, the head on, the meaty or oily or ugly fish, although this process is still ongoing. Now, a sardine, say, blackened over fire and served with perhaps a green herb sauce and some toast to smush everything into and to help the bones go down, is an excellent thing, if done well at the height of summer, with perhaps a glass, far too dry and far too cold, of cheap white wine. The problem, though, is that it has to be done well – and it has to be the height of summer.

A poached salmon, garnished as above, similarly belongs to a hot day, all tennis and strawberries and white flannel, but in general I think poached fish is transitional – it belongs, particularly, to spring, the best time for clear soups and lukewarm food. Just as a perfect spring day is easier to come by than a perfect summer one (because a shower enlivens rather than ruins it, because everything is a bright pale green, because you have a jumper on), so poaching fish well is easier than grilling it – far easier, in fact. Fish cookery always seemed like something of a dark art to me, requiring constant vigilance, open fire, pans of an impeccable non-stick-ness, or uniquely designed and shaped fish kettles – a standard one for your salmon, a wide shield-shape for your prize turbot, a multitude of lithenesses for eels – but it turns out that it is actually extremely easy. Properly shaped and close-fitting kettles are nice if you have the means of heating them properly, and if you are using the resulting broth as part of your dish it is good to not have too much extraneous water, but assuming you aren't cooking a garden-party-sized salmon or a monstrous pike, all you actually need is a pan, into which you put the fish and some water and let it get hot. The flesh of fish, as well as cooking more coldly than meat, also cooks more simply.

When we refer to prime cuts of meat, we tend to mean those that are easy to cook, that don't require hours of careful braising or, conversely, seconds of extreme heat, that are more or less edible at various stages of doneness; by this reckoning, the hidden, lazy fillets and loins are prized above the shoulder, the belly, the foot. That such a variety of flesh exists is because the different muscles of land animals are used in different ways and different amounts: some are tough and load-bearing, some fast and reflexive, others really just bulk; some, like the tongue and cheeks of ruminants or the heart of anything, are in constant motion, others almost static.

Fish – the word fish doesn't really mean anything, or rather it means too much, but I am talking here mainly about the round fish, with skeletons and fins and so on, which you probably picture when you hear the word 'fish' – are completely different. For one thing, completely surrounded by water, they don't need to support their own weight in the way that we do; for another, they are a completely different shape from most other things, but especially from the extremely narrow range of mammals and birds that the majority of humanity eat. Faces apart, mackerel, sardines, hake, cod, pollack, coley, mullet, gurnard and so on – even eels, which aside from their snakey length live well-travelled and deeply mysterious lives – most fish, that is, by our definition, are essentially just two lines of muscle with some bone in the middle, the whole devoted to wiggling itself in some fashion through salt or fresh water. The point is, being a fish requires less effort than being an ox, and so aside from the head, a fish will cook the same the whole way through, which is quickly. The flakes of a fillet of fish are its muscle fibres, and heat travels straight through their open texture, which is why all you have to do to cook it is to get it hot – but not too hot.

I suppose that putting something into quite hot water is the easiest way of getting it hot, but not too hot; it's so easy, in fact, that it almost feels like cheating, as if you aren't really contributing anything to the cooking process. You aren't, of course, but then you often aren't, so you may as well learn to live with it. 'Attend well to your work, then step away'. Laozi tells us. I occasionally think that the full sweat-and-brown-and-deglaze-and-reduce ritual of an elaborate braise exists mainly so the cook feels as though they are adding something of themselves to the commingling of ingredients; for a proper Irish stew, as for countless other preparations across the world, all the cook does is put everything in a pan and let it get hot (for quite a long time, in this case) and it is none the worse for that. More important is the worry that the resulting dish might be a little insipid. There is always the question, when poaching something, of what you are cooking – the flesh or the liquid? Which will leak its flavour into which? You don't want to lose too much of the fish to the broth, or the water to work its way into that delicate muscle, so you do something to each.

The question of the water is very easily solved: don't use water. Come to think of it, this might be the point of that Italian proverb; I don't know, having never, as far as I can remember, cooked fish directly in wine – which seems ridiculous now I write it down. I've certainly eaten fish, some sort of flatfish, cooked in wine, and it was very good; you could really taste the wine, which might not be the effect you desire. The obvious solution is to use fish stock, ideally made from the same kind of fish as the one you are using it to poach, which should keep things nicely balanced. On the other hand, this can't really be done with oily fish, as said oils produce a rather foul and fatty brew, but they can, luckily, stand up to sterner flavours, even when simply poached: sharp, deep, fermented flavours. We say that fish is delicate, and then eat it raw with soy sauce and wasabi. Something like a neatly trimmed fillet of mackerel would be excellent if allowed to get hot in the leftover brine from some fermented tomatoes, for example, perhaps diluted a little to reduce the saltiness; poaching a fish which reacts so well to blistering heat might seem counterintuitive, but the result is rather wonderful. Such an objection misses the point, anyway, which is that this process, with tweaks of flavour, can be applied to any fish whatsoever – poach a mackerel and you can poach a gigantic bass or even, I suppose, a basking shark, though I'm not sure you would want to.

If I *was* poaching a neatly trimmed fillet of mackerel, it's probably because I had got hold of one in the first flush of freshness, sleek and red-eyed and firm to the touch, and I would certainly want to keep it that way. Oily fish, as mentioned, spoils very quickly,

even in the time it takes to prepare it; not that it rots, you understand, or at least not to the point where it becomes inedible, but it
loses the particular vigour that drew you to it and determined your
cooking method in the first place. This degradation, experienced
in real time before your hands and your eyes, is sad to see – you
wish you could arrest heat and time. Luckily, to an extent, you can.
Just take some of that cure, the same as we made for the lamb or
salmon or whatever we were curing, spread it out on a tray and put
the mackerel fillets flesh down into the sweetened salt; put the lot
in the fridge for half an hour, then rinse. Half an hour might not
sound like enough time for much in the way of curing to happen,
and indeed it isn't – that's not what you're after. Mackerel treated in
this way will last a little longer than it would if not, but only a little,
and in any case, you're about to cook it. The salting, in addition to
providing a boost of flavour, merely contracts the flesh a little into
itself and removes a little excess water, firming the fish and giving
it greater integrity with which to withstand its bath.

With the mackerel appropriately fortified, the fermented tomato
brine, or perhaps gherkin brine you are cooking it in should be well
diluted, perhaps two parts of it in eight of water, with a dash of
fish sauce or indeed mackerel garum to boost the flavour again and
a good few feathers of dill – you can put the fillets of mackerel in
whatever liquid you like, really. Bring it gently to a slight simmer
and then, putting a lid on the pan and removing it from the heat,
leave the fillets for a few minutes to cook through in the calm
residual warmth. We might hope that such a simple dish can ease us
just as gently into our meal, a bridge between those insistent pickles
and the wilder meat to come.

6

ON COOKING
FISH IN FIRE

The enjoyment of eating fish, it seems to me, is, more than anything else, dependent on location. I don't find it necessary to sit by a pig farm to enjoy a pork pie, and in fact would probably find it quite off-putting, especially if the sun was high and the smell particularly ripe, but I hardly ever eat fish unless I find myself within a stone's throw of the sea, or at least a large, preferably tidal river. Partly, I suppose, this comes from a genuine concern about freshness. We know that fish does not keep long out of the water, and that it is best enjoyed simply and very fresh; unfortunately, the proximity of its source does not guarantee it will be the freshest, or even fresh at all. So much fish is frozen and shipped back and forth across the world, and whether it's by the sea or anywhere else, we can only trust that our hosts are serving us good things. No, the tendency to eat fish by the sea, I think, comes more from a general aesthetic sense than from any real, practical concerns, a certain longing for terroir, for a connection between the food that we eat and the air we are breathing, which is so often lacking in our over-civilized lives. And when that air already carries salt water and the indefinable smell of the sea, so much the better; it seasons our fish for us, just as the smoke does. The beach and the barbecue go hand in hand, and the affinity of the latter for the produce of the former is no surprise, though any fire, any direct flame, will certainly improve your fish.

By the bridge of the Golden Horn in Istanbul, between the water and a ramshackle line of warehouses, garages and hardware shops, with the general appearance of a place tourists don't go to, there are a number of little restaurants and stalls which sell almost exclusively fish. Huddled together, the seating of one spills into another, and it is difficult from map or signage or really anything to tell them apart; you just need to go to the grill that smells the best, with a good array of spices next to it, and order there – specifically, a *balik ekmek*, which is what you came here for. *Balik ekmek* just means fish bread, a fish sandwich, but the bread is always a softish white roll, similar to a sub or a hero, or to the stuff that Americans call 'French', and the fish is always a fillet of horse mackerel, something we don't really eat in Britain, but much prized by the Japanese, the Portuguese and indeed the Stamboulites, all great appreciators of the whole spectrum of fish and seafood. You might also hear it called scad, but under whatever name, it normally finds its way back into the sea as bait; plain old mackerel is, where I am, the usual defeatist substitute, but perhaps you can badger your fishmonger about getting some – I am certainly trying. Anyway, the fish is grilled, skin-side down over hot coals, with the whitening flesh sprinkled with mild Turkish pepper flakes, perhaps a little sumac and salt (of course) as it cooks, and the sandwich is finished with red cabbage dressed in lemon and the plainest of lettuces. It is one of the world's great sandwiches, up there with the French dip, the *muffaletta*, the *porchetta panino*, the *banh mi*, the beef and horseradish, and if it owes some of that accolade to its location, down by the boats and the bright sea, it owes as much to the mackerel's crisp skin and to the lingering smell of smoke and charcoal.

A lot of fish cookery in professional kitchens, at least those lacking wood- or charcoal-fired heat, is done under the salamander, a large, powerful overhead grill; the domestic equivalent might do, if you let it get good and hot first. Again, this is easily done, and nothing in the way of special equipment is required. Just put your fish, a fat mackerel, say, on a tray, perhaps on a sheet of baking parchment to stop it sticking, oil it and season it inside and out, then put it under the grill and leave it there until it is cooked. If the mackerel is particularly fat, you may want to slash its sides in a few places to allow the heat to penetrate, and perhaps turn the fish over halfway through, although this can be a risky business. In any case, timings are useless, or nearly so; they depend on the size and the freshness of your fish, the development of its muscle in life, and its precise state of rigour since, as well as its exact temperature and that of your grill. Far better to learn how to tell if it is cooked than to bother yourself with so many minutes per side. So, you poke the flesh to one side of the spine, just behind the head, the 'loin' on larger fish; it should give easily to the pressure of your finger. Cut into the same place and you will see that the muscle has turned from translucent to opaque, and from slick and wet on its way to dry, almost grainy. Take a look inside the belly cavity (yes, you should have gutted it) to check for the same things. Although fashion, as well as official safety advice, changes constantly on such matters, you can consider something cooked, really, when you would be happy to eat it; you just need to work out when that is. The trend at the moment is for scorched mackerel, where the skin of a raw or cured fillet is briefly blowtorched, the delicacy of uncooked flesh contrasting with the bitter touch of fire. I'm not really sure about this; I tend to the opinion that you should either cook something or not, but at any rate, this isn't something you'd want to do to a whole fish, not least because you are unlikely to serve one raw. If nothing else, it would be quite hard to get off the bone.

One reason why oily fish respond so well to grilling is that the oils keep them from drying out; the other is the nature of their skin. The thicker hides of white or semi-oily fish, bream or bass for example, are not especially edible when boiled or uncooked, and need an even browning to make them crispy and pleasant to eat; even then, a lot of people push it to the side of their plate, with memories, perhaps, of the soggy skin inside a chip-shop batter. The beautiful stripes of a mackerel, on the other hand, while they don't mind boiling or careful roasting, do very well under flickering flame, blistering here, charring there, nearly untouched in places, their varied imperfection a great part of their charm and certainly fun to eat, crisp shards against the soft, meaty flesh. Naturally well flavoured and seasoned with smoke and flame, what you have here is in itself quite complex; it's a whole animal, for one thing. Nevertheless, it's nice to have a little something on the side. I like to get a large flat pan extremely hot, then roll some crunchy early tomatoes (not the juicy ones of high summer) around it in a little oil so their skins blacken and blister to match the mackerel's, then toss a load of chopped parsley, dill or mint into the pan with the tomatoes, so the leaves stick to the heat and the oil, and to serve all this alongside the whole grilled fish, with perhaps a pickled chilli or two, to remind me of Istanbul and of the bright open sea.

There you have it, then. The anomaly of deep oil aside, those are the two universal methods for cooking anything: essentially, either with or without water, you introduce it to heat until it is cooked. There is no great mystery to the process, no secret known only to the community of chefs and passed down, in hushed tones, in the lightless basements of hotels, restaurants, cafeterias and canteens; all you do is do the above, a lot. I suppose it's that last part that makes the difference. I often think that recipes, particularly those that involve a great deal of manual dexterity, such as laminated pastries and wet-doughed breads, neat carving or butchery, quick-thinking emulsions and pasta sauces, should have as their final instruction: 'repeat one hundred times, or until you can do it perfectly, when tired, hungover, ill, depressed, stressed, panicking or rushed'. Without that last step, they can never be accurate. If you become stuck on a recipe, or frustrated by your apparent inability to follow the simplest set of instructions to create the most basic or time-tested dish, remember, firstly, that the author may have done this a hundred times and had the first fifty come out badly; remember, too, that it is their job to communicate this experience to you, to explain as if to a child the steps, which have become second nature to them, the pitfalls, the hard parts and the pauses, the breath and the rhythm of the recipe as you follow it from beginning to end; remember, lastly, how easy it was to poach that fish, how it just warmed through until it was cooked, and that almost anything, however ugly, however much it unattractively flops around the bowl or around the plate, can be edible if you just look after it carefully through the heat, and season it well.

7

ON BOILING AND NOT BOILING VEGETABLES

Now I want to talk about the products not of rivers, but of rain: plants, which are, when it comes down to it, mostly water anyway. And in Britain we often cook them in more of it. You'll notice that the liquid we're cooking with has, so far, barely reached a simmer, and certainly not a full-blown boil, which I suppose it might now be time for. Cooking styles go in and out of fashion, like anything else. Once, as we saw, the slow stew was the preferred way of cooking vegetables, if only accidentally; more recently, steaming was considered the ideal method of keeping flavour and vitamins inside. When I was learning to cook, the blanch-and-shock was in; now I tend to follow the Italian way, allowing the vegetables to braise gently, then gradually settle to room temperature. These methods all have their value — apart, perhaps, from stewing and then discarding the cooking water — so the one you choose depends on what you want out of your vegetables. It strikes me that the French-restaurant method of cooking green things — a plunge into briskly boiling water, a few minutes' cooking, a plunge into iced water, a toss through hot butter (or a waltz through the microwave) to serve — is, in common with a lot of French-restaurant techniques, much more about appearance and texture than it is about flavour. The first green flush of broccoli, for example, meaning that heat has only just transformed and penetrated it, and that the stalk retains that brisk snap to the teeth, is a fine thing, and looks well on a plate, but it barely tastes of broccoli. You get much more flavour out of a dully muted brassica than a still-perky one, which just goes to show that there is a difference between food that looks nice, and food that looks like it tastes nice. Still, it's not all about flavour, is it? We eat with our eyes, or so they say; thankfully not literally.

Let's say you want some bright green, nicely textured vegetables. Perhaps you think they might make a good contrast to some sort of gamey meat, and that with a strong, pungent dressing, it doesn't particularly matter if they haven't fully grown into their own flavour; fair enough. Put a big pan of water on to boil, your biggest pan, unless that is a stockpot or a gigantic preserving pan. You are trying to cook as quickly and as consistently as possible, so you want the temperature of the water to barely drop when you introduce the vegetables to it; this means, essentially, you need lots of it (the same principle applies to deep-frying). So, a big pan, two-thirds full of water, a fair amount of salt – you could just as well be cooking pasta, so pay attention, even if you don't intend to ever blanch and shock your vegetables. While the water is coming to the boil, do whatever you intend to do to the greens, which might involve separating broccoli into florets and trimming off the hardest parts of the stalk, perhaps halving the largest ones; cutting off the tail ends, destringing and slicing beans into appropriately sized pieces; separating leaf and stalk of chard, large spinach or kale; removing the cores and shuffling out the leaves of savoy or pointed spring cabbages... I don't know. These are your hypothetical vegetables, not mine. Some people shred leeks and blanch them as greens, a shocking treatment of a wonderful allium, which responds so well to slow cooking. A leek should never crunch.

You should have a lid for your pan, to help it reach the required violent boil, and you should also remove it from time to time, to see what's going on in there and to watch the water go through the various stages of heating – the eddies and swirls, the lifts and falls and whirlpools; we looked at them before but it's good to remind yourself. As your panful approaches readiness, make sure you have what you need for the next stage, whether you're cooking greens or pasta – a spider or sieve and a sink full of cold water and ice for the former; a cup to scoop out some of the cooking water, warm bowls, cheese and dressing or sauce, all waiting for the latter. If there is one thing that a home cook can learn from a professional kitchen, it is to always be prepared for what is going to happen next.

Now, depending on how big your pan is and how long you have fussed over your vegetables, the water should be approaching its boiling point, which means, when you take a look, that it should be foaming and pushing against the lid's constraint, and that the edges should be rising and falling into the middle in a constant wave or roll, the whole thing as expressive of heat and motion as the surface of an active volcano. This being so, drop in your greens, or rather slide them in, the edge of the container they are in touching the face of the water. Recipes often ask you to drop or throw or slap things into other hot things, as if the quickness and violence of the cooking requires a matching violence from the cook; this, obviously, is not the case. If a professional cook drops, throws, slaps, slams down pans and whirls plates around, that is largely because, firstly, they have read too much Anthony Bourdain, and secondly because they are hot, tired, spend all day on their feet, and know they have to cook another fifty plates of food before they can sit down again. It's certainly not because it speeds up their work in any way; or if it does, as in squeezing steak down into a hot pan, it does so to the detriment of the end product – which, it's true, might be the last thing on the mind of the professional cook as they go about their day. This is why large kitchens have someone whose job it is to finish and check each plate before it goes out into the world, a final proof of the pudding before the eating. You, presumably, don't have such a person, and your first critic will be your diners – so slow down, pay attention, and slide green vegetables gently into hotly rolling water. Let it come back to the boil, which shouldn't take very long if there is enough water. Now, at this point most recipes will specify some arbitrary number of minutes for which to boil your vegetables, which rather assumes that you're going to set a timer and do something else for the duration. We, on the other hand, are going to watch.

There is no magic formula for calculating how long exactly a vegetable is going to take to cook. So much depends on the age of the plant, when it was picked, how long it has sat in your fridge, your cupboard or your vegetable rack; different varieties and crops from different times of year will have different densities and quantities of water within. I also have no idea what veg you are cooking. The steady march of efficiency and consistency has standardized a lot of these things, it's true; most of the animals we buy to eat have been homogenized to an extraordinary degree, and much fresh produce, even in markets and greengrocers, comes from the vast polytunnels of Holland and Spain. If you buy nice vegetables, though, grown seasonally in the ground, there will be an element of chance in cooking them, and you just have to observe and decide yourself when they are cooked. That, after all, is what whoever wrote the recipe you might have been following did, assuming they tested it properly at all – they didn't weigh and measure each broccoli stalk to work out exactly how long it would take for hot water to penetrate it; they looked, poked and squeezed.

There is a point when a green vegetable takes on a colour that is more vivid and lifelike than it was when growing and, like the lamb you may or may not have made earlier, starts to resemble itself if painted in oils; that is the point you are looking for when, for some reason, we say that it is blanched – in fact it is flooded with colour. It is useful, when cooking vegetables, to have to hand a small, pointed knife, perhaps one of those little ones with a bird-beaked blade, with which to prod; assuming you have one, do this now. The point of the blade should slip easily into the hardest and thickest part of the vegetable with only a little effort. If you are cooking something particularly leafy, it can be hard to test with a knife, in which case fish out a bit with spider, sieve or tongs, rinse under cold water, and take a little nip of it with your incisors; in both cases, 'yielding' should be the word that comes to mind. If it does, then the cooking needs to stop. Scoop the greens out of the pan, quickly but not violently, and straight into the waiting iced water, ready for draining and whatever else you are going to do to them. Now, in an old-fashioned French kitchen, vegetables treated this way would probably be re-heated in a little emulsion of butter and water, boiled up together, in which case you would need to arrest the initial cooking slightly before we did. This means you need to learn what your chosen vegetables look like just – but only just – before they are cooked, and if that seems to you like a culinary koan, well it does to me, too. Frankly, I wouldn't bother.

Just the other day I was reading a thirteenth-century Buddhist work called *Instructions for the Zen Cook*. Ostensibly a deep spiritual guide disguised as a practical manual for the cooks at Zen monasteries (always monks themselves), it does in fact contain a great deal of useful advice for the professional cook, although following it as a cookbook might get a little confusing. Among its many aphorisms, the majority of which counsel care, preparation and a quiet reverence for even the plainest ingredients, it suggests the reader, as 'a teacher of men and of heavenly beings, make[s] the best use of whatever greens you have'. Good advice, it seems to me, so obvious it barely needs stating – but as it has been, let's look at it a little more. The first way to make the best use of your greens, or indeed any other ingredients, is to look, specifically, at the ones you have. Don't start cooking regular calabrese broccoli wishing that it was purple sprouting, or purple sprouting wishing that it was asparagus, or cabbage wishing it was anything else at all; it won't get you anywhere. Yes, you can cook them all in similar ways, but it doesn't mean you should. Even if you do, they don't all taste the same. Purple sprouting broccoli fills a similar seasonal niche to asparagus, it's true, and both respond as well to grilling or roasting as they do to the more traditional boil, but the presence of one in the depths of winter and the other in the first flush of British summer, as well as the fact they have quite distinct flavours, means they naturally partner with different things – though both are very happy, as we all are, with a soft-boiled egg.

So, although I have given you a guide to the cooking of all green things, treating them, as old-fashioned kitchens often did, as one homogenous mass, you should really only pick your cooking method when you have your vegetables in hand, and tailor it as much to them as to your recipe. Having done this, you can proceed to the second way of making the best use of them, which is to execute your chosen method as well as you can; that is to say, you should ignore the cooking instructions given above, or at least the second half of them. Blanch, but never shock.

8

ON DRESSING
GREENS WITH
ANCHOVY

Taking into account the attention that needs to be paid to the star of the show, making a sauce or dressing for pasta or broccoli is really the only other thing you should be doing during its cooking time. For this reason, pasta sauces should take either hours to make and be left to sit overnight before re-heating as you cook, or a few minutes. An excellent slow-cooked ragù notwithstanding, most of my favourite pasta sauces are of the 'minutes' school. *Cacio e pepe* – cheese and pepper – has recently become popular as a quick and simple pasta dressing, but it is quite tricky to make. If the amount of cooking water, or the temperature of the cheese or the bowl is just off, you end up with a clotted, stringy mess – which is probably a good thing, or I would eat it all the time. My go-to, quick pasta dressing is oil, garlic and chilli, the second two cooked in the first until the garlic starts to brown, then cooled off with a squeeze of lemon juice and tossed through hot spaghetti with, of course, Parmesan, or more often Grana Padano. Just as good, though not really a sauce at all, is lots of finely shredded cabbage added for the last minute of the pasta's cooking time (in contrast to vegetables, I always time pasta; you just have to take two minutes off whatever the packet says), the whole brought together with a good splash of oil and even more cheese and black pepper than usual. An anchovy or two is always welcome in such quick 'sauces', giving the kind of backbone you only usually find in day-long braises; this applies equally to dressings for green vegetables.

These things come and go, in and out of favour, but it is to be hoped that the anchovy retains its current place as the seasoning of choice for bitter green vegetables – and all green vegetables are more or less bitter. They used to be much more so, in fact. All brassicas descend ultimately from wild seashore vegetables, the sea-broccolis and sea-cabbages and so on which can still be found all around the British coastline, and which retain much more of a mustard quality than do their cultivated relative. Inland, meanwhile, you can find dandelions and jack-by-the-hedge and various leaves of hedgerow and field, from which derive chicories and spinach and such-like, all of them bitter, too bitter, in general, for our modern British palate.

In Italy, they have a much higher tolerance of bitter flavours. Perhaps, bitter so often being an indication of poison, this is a legacy of the Borgias; or perhaps it is more to do with olives, which in their raw, fresh state are mouth-puckeringly inedible, and even fully processed, brined for many weeks, are challenging for the first few tries. I read once that this is because they are one of the few chemically alkali things we eat; this may be true when raw, and certainly the caustic lye they are often treated in is, but as the final product, fermented and acidifed, is most definitely not, I'm not sure where this assertion came from.

At any rate, the continued consumption of olives has accus-tomed the Italian national palate, if there is such a thing, to very bitter flavours. Espresso coffee is perhaps the most obvious example, alongside the vast array of bitter liqueurs which form the Italian cocktail cupboard, Fernet, Cynar, Campari and Aperol being the best known, though it would be a mistake to think that this sophisticated taste is confined to adults. The fizzy drink Chinotto is flavoured with the same bitter citrus as Campari, and people of all ages eat piles and piles of bitter greens, chicories and radicchios and brassicas of all shapes and hues, raw or braised or boiled, but always quite heavily dressed and often served at a warm room temperature, which is by far the nicest way to eat such things. In many trattorias, in fact, they seem to cook their vegetables at the start of service, dress them while still warm, and then leave them out, gleaming with olive oil, for you to admire and to pick from for your antipasti or your *contorno*. It is a shame that, in Britain, antipasti has come to mean endless plates of charcuterie, sun-dried tomatoes, and other things better suited to serving with a stiff drink. In the south of Italy at least, antipasti are often just great plates of greens – artichokes, peppers, white beans and the like – all well-cooked and dressed according to their needs, an approach to vegetable-eating we would do well to learn from.

In hotter countries they tend to be less obsessed with piping hot food than we are, which means that not only can they develop a greater appreciation of flavour – taste being erratic at higher temperatures – but that they can do more to the food on its way to being served; the two things go hand in hand, I suppose. If you insist on your greens being still-steaming as they arrive at the table, for example, then you can't give them much more than a bath in already-hot butter. If you have a more relaxed approach to such things, you can toss them, still warm, in a dressing whose punchy ingredients will settle and calm as they seep into your vegetables.

Back, then, to the anchovy. When I talk about anchovies, I am referring to the brown, salted and aged fillets that come packed in oil in jars or tins; you do sometimes find whole salted anchovies here, but they are rare, as indeed are fresh ones. A lingering prejudice, I think, surrounds these little fishes, as if something from the sea has no business seasoning something from the land or sky, which is ridiculous. Nobody objects to a little bacon in their chowder, unless for religious or ethical reasons. Although people often describe anchovies as very fishy, they don't really taste of the sea any more, except in the sense that they are salty and, I suppose, deeply flavoured; they've been away from the sea for too long for that. You can add quite a lot of anchovies to a pan of braising ox cheeks or a roasting leg of lamb, and no-one will complain that the result tastes fishy; they'll compliment you, rather, on the depth of umami, the long-lasting flavour you have attained, or at least they will if they have any manners. No, a brown anchovy tastes like a brown anchovy, nothing more or less, and as such it makes an excellent seasoning for boiled green vegetables, particularly the more bitter ones; extreme flavours like each other's company.

So you might have kale, or large-leafed dandelion chicory, the sort of thing that sees you through the first snap of winter; you might, months later, have beautifully pale spring cabbages; and there is always chard. Always. But let's say that you have broccoli of some sort, purple sprouting if you like, and that it is late in the season, the start of spring, and the wild garlic is out, carpeting bluebell woods with its wide plangent leaves. That seems a good time to be cooking, and anchovy, which goes well with garlic in all forms, goes especially well with the wild green-leaved sort, which often seems to find its way into farmers' markets, greengrocers, delis and the like, if you don't have the time or the inclination to go to the woods and seek out the smell. You should, though; it flour-ishes everywhere across the country, with place-names beginning 'Rams-' often an indicator, at least once upon a time, of a good green carpet of these ramsons.

Once your water is on to boil and your broccoli is trimmed of its woodier parts, take a few anchovy fillets and half chop, half smash them across your chopping board, so you end up with some recognizable pieces of fermented fish along with a little brown paste, then scrape all of it into a bowl. Clean knife and board of anchovy oil, then get four or five leaves of wild garlic and a small handful of parsley – the now-standard Italian or flatleaf, for prefer-ence, though curly parsley will do if you cut it fine enough – grate the zest of a lemon over them both and chop everything together with some red chilli flakes, if you like, until the whole lot is deeply fragrant and you can't really tell one leaf from the other. Put this in the bowl, too, then check the water – it's probably ready for your broccoli. To the bowl, add some mustard, red wine vinegar – quite a lot of it – perhaps a pinch of sugar, or even honey if the vinegar isn't very good, and oil, a good, bitter, grassy oil; quite a lot of that, too. Give the whole thing a fairly violent stir. You aren't looking for emulsification, at least not in the full, stable way of mayonnaise; for one thing, oil emulsified into herbs goes a weirdly bright green, and for another, the blades of a food processor, or even the more traditional pounding of a pestle, will bruise the parsley and garlic leaves, bringing out the generic grassiness of greenery at the expense of the individual flavour of each plant. Sometimes you want that, but in this case we don't. The dressing, though not completely amalgamated, should still hang together, with recognizable components suspended in oil; if so, it's ready for the sprouting broccoli to be scooped, with spider or sieve, out of the rolling water and straight into its rich bath, there to sit, the flavours gradually mingling and soaking into the green flesh as it cools to a warm room temperature.

This meal appears to be taking place in the early springtime (it's nice to have a date, isn't it?), but it could really happen at any point in the year. The spear-shaped leaves of wild garlic give way to garlic chives, to the wet new-season garlic and then the dried and separated cloves used all year round; they change in tandem with the broccoli, the spring or the summer cabbage, the chicory of whatever kind, and indeed the lightly dressed vegetables with which, you'll remember, we topped the cured lamb or perhaps trout, somewhere at the start of this meal. What you make the dressing with and how you make it depends on how you feel, the weather, any number of things, as well as the particular ingredients you have available. The point, I think, is to not start pondering recipes until you have your brassica in your hands, ready to put it to the best use that you can. Only then can you decide if your anchovy dressing should be thick and buttery, wet and chunky, or if it should exist at all. Maybe you should fry bread-crumbs in melted anchovies and top your lightly dressed greens in that; maybe you should grill leaves of spring cabbage over open fire and dunk them hot into vinegar infused with dried seaweed for that saline hit of umami. Do as you like, I suppose, or rather do as your ingredients intend to do; they usually know best.

9

ON THE COOKING OF ONIONS

When we look for evidence of life around distant formations of stars, which may in fact have twinkled their last ten thousand years ago, it is mainly water that we look for, clouds or streams or breaths of precious water; where there is water, we think, there must follow life. If this seems a little self-centred, it is understandable, I suppose. We, the surface of this planet, and almost everything we feed ourselves with, are mostly made of water; the elemental act of cooking is chiefly the act of moving water from one place to another. When we cure lamb or salmon fillets, legs of ham, boned-out shoulders, herring, or anything of that sort, we are using the dry salt and ambient temperatures as a way of drawing out water; conversely, when we boil pasta, rice, polenta or any kind of gruel, dried pulses and grains, we are rehydrating as much as cooking; that is to say, moving water from the outside to the inside of these items.

You could say that one of the definitions of that word, 'cook', is to bring something to the point where it cannot hold on to water, where it starts to leak life out into your pan; look at the juices that run out of a roasting chicken, see a piece of lamb shrink as it grills. This is particularly the case with vegetables. If you have ever cooked *peperonata*, *piperade*, *shakshuka*, or any similar dish, which rests on a ragù of sweet peppers, you will remember, I'm sure, a certain sense of frustration. You have these firm, bright peppers, each with their particular flavour and crunch, and pleasant to eat raw – if a little reminiscent of generic salad garnishes on the side of jacket potatoes or toasted sandwiches – and will have taken care, of course, to cut them neatly, to remove the white ribs and the clusters of seeds, which are curiously hard under a knife. Then you add them to hot oil and all your effort is wasted. Nothing seems to happen to them – or if it does, it's bad. There is a point, it seems to me, between uncooked and fully cooked, where fruit, in particular, are at the absolute nadir of their flavour. A raw tomato (at least a good one) is herbal, fruity and brisk; even a substandard one, if cooked for a very long time in a very low oven, covered with good oil, becomes intense, jammy and savoury. Think, on the other hand, of the grilled breakfast tomato: cooked just enough to reach that point where all the fresh flavour is destroyed, too hot to taste what is left, mealy and watery, without the chance to develop the full potential of its cooked flavour... It's no wonder so many people don't like tomatoes – they have too often consumed them only in the form of a travesty. Plums are the same, and so, definitely, are peppers. Cooking them properly takes time.

You need to cook peppers long enough for their walls to collapse and for their juices to leak out, which, the first few times you do it, takes at least ten minutes longer than you think it is going to; very often this is because the recipe you are following has lied to you. Most recipes are rather coy about the actual time it takes to cook vegetables. Anyway, you'll know when your peppers are properly cooked, assuming you are cooking peppers, because when the juices begin to flow out they do so very suddenly; your pan will turn a solid rusty red, and the peppers themselves will deflate by about two-thirds. This, I suppose, may be a reason why cooks are reluctant to either fully cook their peppers themselves or to instruct other people to do so; for one thing, it takes twice as long, and for another, you need twice as many ingredients. No-one wants their recipe to be the most extravagant – unless that is exactly their aim, I guess, in which case peppers probably won't be involved – and time is all too often of the essence in modern recipe-writing. Of course we need convenience, efficiency, a meal on the table in half an hour, but all that at the expense of flavour is counterproductive. What use, after all, is a quick meal that no-one enjoys?

Nowhere is this pernicious doctrine of speed more evident than in the case of the onion. This singularly useful allium is one of the many vegetables, along with various spices, animals, cooking techniques and so on, which the Romans spread around the outposts of their Empire during that entity's chequered history. Now, of course, it is ubiquitous, from the Straits of Gibraltar all around the wide Mediterranean Sea, up through Northern and Eastern Europe, into Russia and beyond. Everything starts with an onion, sliced, diced, grated, brunoised, burnt, crushed, roasted or raw, but most often cooked quite gently in a little oil, pig or beef or sheep fat, whole or clarified butter, perhaps in the company of a few other select vegetables, which seem to change across Europe and beyond in a sort of stepwise puzzle, each country sharing two of three or four vegetables with its neighbour, one of which is always the onion. The others might be leek, carrot, celery, celeriac, green or red pepper, parsley root, bulb fennel, garlic, cabbage, tomato – whatever the combination, it will be the bedrock of that country's cuisine, rejoicing, perhaps, under the name of *mirepoix*, *sofrito*, *soffritto* or *włoszczyzna*, which, it should be said, I have no idea how to pronounce.

The mirepoix, the French variation on this theme, is seemingly considered the correct or original version, and the others as minor corruptions; or we could say that mirepoix has become the British word for it too. Whatever you want to call it, people invariably try to complicate it. I once watched a chef demonstrate the construction of a game ragù at a local food festival. I always start a ragù, he said, with what I call the 'Holy Trinity': red onion, white onion, celery, carrots, leeks and garlic. I don't recall if he added anything else to this list. Now, I am impressed by the palate that can discern both red and white onions in the depths of a game ragù, but this aside, it seems obvious that this chef had heard a soffritto (as would be appropriate to Italian cuisine) referred to in this fashion, and in calling his own six-ingredient medley the 'Holy Trinity', never paused to consider either the actual meaning of the words he was using or, more importantly, the deeper meaning of that phrase, which is that the perfect simplicity of three ingredients is in fact all that is required when you begin the construction of a game or, more specifically, a rabbit ragù. Anything extra does not add to but rather muddies the waters you are attempting to clarify.

Three ingredients are all you need – even, or perhaps especially, if you are then going to add a dozen more. Onion, carrot and celery; that should do it. Each of these vegetables brings its own particular quality to the table and you really don't need, for example, three different alliums in one stew. I recently read, in fact, that Italian cooks will never – *never* – use garlic and onion in the same dish, which is certainly untrue; more believably, I have also read that it is a Neapolitan convention not to mix the two in a soffritto. I'm not sure whether this has anything to do with flavour at all; it seems more likely to be a legacy of medieval medical advice around the dangers of overheating the body's humours with fiery foods. The fact that this tradition has survived to be repeated, however, is indicative of the seriousness with which the Italians take simplicity, and, indeed, their food. On a more personal note, I don't really see the point of garlic unless you are going to use a lot of it. In particularly long braises I will add an entire head, the cloves separated and peeled but left whole, little garlicky treats in a rich meaty tangle; I don't really think this is the place for that, though. Let the onion do the hard work – it is, after all, very versatile.

The phrase 'know your onions' is, I often think, no coincidence; there is certainly a lot to learn. Non-professional cooks, I find, tend to dislike the preparation of onions, at least in large amounts. This is partly, I'm sure, because they haven't had enough practice (or don't use a big or sharp enough knife), but it is also because they are using the wrong onions. Most of the onions you buy here are, perhaps unsurprisingly, English brown onions, and they are both quite small and quite pungent, as onions go. Pointlessly pungent, in fact, since in most situations involving standard onions, you will want to cook most of the strength and acid out of them before introducing much else to the mix. If you use English onions to make even a decent soffritto, let alone a *pissaladière*, a French onion soup, a *salsa Genovese* or *sarde in saor*, then the amount you need will make you cry twice, once when you are peeling them and again when you are slicing. There is really no need for this; cooking should not make you weep, at least with pain. Professional kitchens tend to use the large Spanish onion, a little milder, perhaps, than the English, but more importantly, about three times the size. Remember that onions are one of the three foundations of your dish, and remember, furthermore, that when cooked properly, they will lose a lot of their bulk to the air. With this in mind, think how much onion your dish needs; it is quite a lot, generally.

I often use the large Italian onions, wrapped in their papery white skins. These are especially mild, well suited to pickling and fermenting, to light macerations and salting, as well as to fierce grilling and to long, drawn-out cooking; if onion is one of the primary ingredients of your dish, I'd advise you to use these. A tortilla, for example, of the Spanish variety, which is made almost entirely of potato and golden, well-cooked onion, held together with only a little egg, is the perfect home for these, when prepared properly. In this context, this means that they should first be halved, from the root to the tip, the skin peeled away and the ends squared off, then sliced along the length, as finely as you can – ideally paper-thin and translucent, but don't worry if not, just try harder next time. Slicing this way allows the flesh of the onion to break and cook down into an almost jammy mass, if that is what you are after; slicing the other way, into half-moons across the rings, is generally best for pickles and marinades. Now, the hard work done, you have the pleasure of actually cooking them. A tortilla or a French onion soup requires you to cook the onion almost to melting point, until, their physicality nearly gone, they are almost all flavour – hence the thinness of our slicing.

The cooking of a soffritto is a little more restrained and demands a slightly different technique. Halve the onions in the same way, but, having peeled them, square off only the tip, leaving the root end intact. Place each half cut-side down with the hairy root pointing away from you and slice down the onion in a rounded arch, then turn the whole around so the cuts now go from right to left and cut across them until the whole falls apart into little pieces.

I'm not sure there is anything better than the smell of onions gently sweating in butter. I was obsessed with it when I started to cook, trying to capture and prolong it as far as possible, trying to get as much of it as I could into the finished dish. The smell is nearly complete in itself, a heady oxymoron of fat and acid, carrying both deep savoury tones and a hint of sweetness which nods towards the dark caramel browns of that onion soup, but more than anything it is the smell of possibility. Think of all the things those onions could grow up to be! It can be hard to pin them down to just one dish, but you must, there is cooking to be done.

Now forget that tortilla for a moment – forever, in fact; it wasn't destined to exist – and return to our soffritto.

10

ON WILD AND DOMESTIC CELERIES

To clarify, then, we have four onions, ideally large, white-skinned and Italian, four fat and woody carrots, and four sticks of good celery. Celery, more than most things, or at least more than most vegetables, seems to consist mainly of water, and occupies the curious position of being apparently both bland and divisive; it is one of my favourite vegetables. When in season, which is not when our meal is taking place, unfortunately, Fenland celery, huge and leafy and still wearing its earthy cloak, is an excellent treat and worthy of a place at the centre of the table. If I come across this or any of similar quality, I normally take my cue from the Sicilians, who grow excellent celery and braise it with wine vinegar, enough honey to balance the vinegar, perhaps some capers and mint, and serve the whole at room temperature as an accompaniment to poached or grilled fish. I've never seen Sicilian celery for sale here, but even the fairly bland Spanish stuff that is available year-round is good if peeled, finely diced and mixed with chopped green olives and mint into a salsa, or if used as one of the three keystones of our soffritto. If the bitter herbal notes are less pronounced than they might be, at least they are there.

There is something ancient-seeming about celery, with its particular delicacy, elusive and at the same time utterly unmistakable, especially when used as a spice in the form of celery seed or the more familiar celery salt (part of its own holy trinity, with vodka and tomato, in the form of a Bloody Mary; Worcestershire and Tabasco sauces don't count as extra ingredients, as they come under the heading of seasonings). Celery seed was a mainstay of the ancient Roman storecupboard, often turning up in those pounded mixtures I mentioned earlier, alongside the garum, vinegar, honey, mustard and silphium, with which everything, seemingly, was flavoured. If the plant itself is alive and well, and indeed still farmed in many places across the world, the spice instead seems to wear the aura of those lost tastes, victims of changes in fashion, in climate, in our palates or, as in the case of silphium, simply of human depredation, as the Romans found the plant so delicious that they ate it to extinction, robbing the world of its flavour. Spices and herbs are, it seems to me, often the most distinctive of ingredients at our disposal: while all meat, broadly speaking, tastes like meat, all fish certainly tastes like fish, and even vegetables from different parts of different plants, grown above or below the ground, seem to partake of a general vegetal quality, each herb and spice is its own little world. Of course you have your mints, your aniseeds, the woody and medicinal, the floppy and fresh, but, still, each one is subtly different; cooking with a new spice for the first time, whether blue fenugreek, sumac, marigold, pink pepper, dense smoked chilli or perfumed caraway, can seem like discovering a new colour.

Silphium was already starting to disappear, or rather, to be destroyed, by the time the great Roman cookbook *Apicius* was compiled; perhaps it had already gone. At any rate, it was still in living memory, and the suggested substitution of asafoetida, with its strong, savoury, almost sweaty smell of onions, might give us some indication of how silphium may have tasted; equally, of course, it might not. Perhaps asafoetida is similar only in that it is strong, or rather foetid, as the name implies; perhaps the modern plant tastes nothing like it did a couple of thousand years ago; perhaps the Romans, their palates used to sourer wine, more bitter leaves, more aged or exotic animals, tasted something different in it to what we taste now; we'll never know. The fact is that a particular taste, prized around the civilized, or at least the Roman world, has, thanks to the onward march and greed of an expanding empire, disappeared entirely from the face of the earth, never to be savoured again; and who knows what else, across the dry land or in the weighty depths of the oceans, we are close to losing. Not celery, that's for sure, even if we are losing a taste for the extremes of its flavour.

To achieve those pale-green stems and their juicy crunch, the farmed celery plants are blanched; not in the culinary sense, you understand (though they may later be), but in the sense of being whitened. Like good early rhubarb and winter endives, they are robbed of light, the Fenland or Spanish or Sicilian mud packed up around them, so the stalks plump up, never maturing into bitter greenness, full instead to the brim with water. Left to themselves, celery plants are much darker and leafier, the stalks spindly and very stringy; similar, as you might expect, to the wild varieties and their relatives Alexanders, which have become a popular foraged ingredient.

*

Now, whatever your feelings about the current trend for wild food, its admirable back-to-nature spirit, its pretentious one-upmanship, its bold bypassing of a broken food industry or its undeniable and unmanaged effect on local ecosystems, Alexanders (one of those words which is both a singular and a plural) are a fairly unproblematic example, at least if you go and get them yourself. One of our suppliers offers foraged items, in their various seasons, among them Alexanders and bagfuls of nettles; as these are both common and easily identifiable, this seems a little pointless to me. I suppose we might as well eat nettles, if they are there, but I'd rather have spinach, while Alexanders are easy enough to get for yourself. They are particularly abundant in coastal Suffolk, and when they are in season they are everywhere, in hedgerows, on clifftops and covering odd little clearings in the woods. The season lasts a while, depending on what you want to do with them; the whole plant is edible, and while the usefulness of the stalks disappears as they grow older and stringy, the leaves are pretty much always good, with a strong, astringent herbal twang. They are reminiscent, certainly, of parsley, celery and the like, but (as with all herbs) possess a certain something all of their own.

This certain something, as is often the case, is shown to excellent effect in a good green sauce, a herbal affair that has been gradually taking over from heavier, perhaps cream- or butter-based concoctions as the go-to sauce of British restaurant kitchens. *Salsa verde*, in the original Italian, is often used to perk up long-boiled or plainly grilled meats, but green sauce can also be of service on top of soups and game ragùs, nestled among a sort-of Sunday roast, or even as a sandwich spread. It is a useful thing, in other words, to have up your sleeve.

Now, green sauce is one of those things that everybody has their own recipe for, and every recipe is considered to be the correct one; I prefer to see it as a set of loose guidelines adhering to a sort of general theory of green sauce – except, of course, that it must always, but always, be chopped by hand. A food processor pulverizes; a pestle smashes; a good knife slices neatly through perky leaves, keeping the clean, individual flavour of each herb distinct, and maintaining a certain crunch throughout. The method agreed on, then, the ingredients can be played around with. There should always be herbs, of course, a lot of herbs – more than you can reasonably buy from a supermarket. You want a whole bunch, say, of parsley, from a greengrocer or a little Turkish cornershop, at least 100 grams of it, and you want to pick the leaves from the stems one by one, unless the stems are very fine indeed – which they generally aren't unless you buy your herbs from the supermarket. Whatever else you use, parsley should make up at least half the bulk of the sauce. A sauce made chiefly from mint might be green, at least for a short while, but it isn't a green sauce. If I'm making one from Alexanders or celery leaf, I normally use half flatleaf parsley and half of the stronger herb, though you could use less; some people feel the need to add mint, dill, or even tarragon to the mix, which seems to me to have more to do with the one-dimensional nature of commercially farmed herbs than with anything else. Use parsley and Alexanders and you have enough going on, at least as far as herbs go.

To the herbs, which should be chopped finely but not too finely, you will need to add oil, good bitter olive oil (without which it wouldn't be a sauce), garlic, crushed, in some fashion, to a fine paste; and anchovies, chopped or crushed as you like, just a couple of fillets to give the whole thing some authority. Those are the four essentials, but you will also feel the need for salt – at least to help you crush the garlic – and some vinegar, preferably a sweetish red wine vinegar, to balance the oil's bitterness, tame the pungent anchovies, and generally to round things out. The thing as a whole should be grassy, it should be sharp, it should above all be herbal, and it should hit you with all of those things at once, so it is down to you really to adjust the amounts of the various ingredients in order to find a suitable balance. If you think it needs to be sharper, consider adding something pickled to the mix, perhaps a few capers or finely chopped gherkins, both very welcome ingredients to cut through the richness of a slow-cooked rabbit ragù. 'Salsa', of course, just means sauce, and the association of the word with a rough-cut Tex-Mex affair has more to do with our own culinary and linguistic blinkers than with anything inherent in its meaning; despite this, or perhaps because of my own happy memories of those four-pack dips, of which the sour cream and chive was, of course, the best, I like to keep my salsa verde from becoming too sloppy. In partic-ular, although I am quite free with vinegar, I add the oil last and slowly, stopping when there is just enough to bind the whole thing together into something that drops rather than drips off the end of a spoon. This is, you'll note, directly contrary to the traditional Italian advice on dressing a salad.

Our words 'sauce', 'salsa' and 'salad' all come, ultimately, from the Latin for salt or salted, a usage which survives in Greece and the Middle East, where a *salata* is as often a strongly flavoured paste as anything else; think, for example, of taramasalata – cod-roe salad, if you were to directly translate it. It is unclear whether this is because such 'salads' were always made of heavily salted ingredients, for example olives, cheeses, cured meats and fish roe, or because they provided a more general seasoning, an enlivening of an otherwise bland plate, perhaps, of bread, gruel or pulses.

Put the green sauce aside for now, and get on with dicing vegetables. As I was saying, while celery's pale green stalks certainly have no place in a bright green sauce, the vegetable certainly deserves a life beyond immersion, raw, in dips of various kinds, and a soffritto is no bad place for it to end up. If the vegetables within it do lose a certain amount of individuality in the long sweat, and the braise or simmer that inexorably follows, they are still there, in little discernible cubes, and their flavour is everywhere. There is a line in *The Adventures of Huckleberry Finn* in which the title character extols the superior flavours of a bowl of stew, where the initial cooking swaps all the juices around, so everything tastes of and mingles with everything else. Usually taken as a rather heavy-handed metaphor for American culture, this is also an astute analysis of stew, far removed from the traditional assertion that one browns ingredients to be stewed in order to seal in the juices. No, in a stew, a daube, a braise, a tagine or a ragù, we want our flavours to swap and change about, and so, having peeled the outer ribs of our celery and discarded the long strings which result, we dice it finely, to the same thickness as our pieces of onion.

Celery and the like are rather more convenient to chop than onions, firstly because doing so does not make you weep hot tears, and secondly because of their rather more convenient shape – at least when it comes to dicing; it is much harder to form a stick of celery into a ring than an onion, or so I would imagine. All you need to do when it comes to dicing celery is to slice the sticks into thinner sticks, perhaps (depending on the length of your knife) having halved the whole across its middle first, and then, rotating your little woodpile by ninety degrees, cut them across again into little cubes. There is something immensely satisfying about doing this once you get into a rhythm, and when you do you will find yourself dicing things finely as often as possible, especially if you invest in one of those large Chinese cleavers, which act, alongside their obvious purpose, as useful shovels for tidying and moving around your piles of diced vegetables. In Bee Wilson's *Consider The Fork*, which takes a deep look at the utensils with which we eat and cook, she notes, in fact, that the development of these fearsome-looking knives, which are capable of great technical delicacy, followed the development of the neat knifework required to cook quickly but evenly, as in stir-fries and so on. This cooking method was, in turn, a result of the relative scarcity of firewood in China. So while the English burned everything they could find and roasted their oxen whole, the Chinese learned to dice their vegetables evenly, and to cook them as quickly as they could, because they had no choice.

We do have a choice, of course, but the fact that you can leave your vegetables in huge chunks to break down slowly in the braise doesn't mean that you should; in any case, you couldn't call such a thing a ragù. A ragù is uniform, yes, but that is from the close texture of careful preparation, not because it is cooked eternally until everything collapses – or if it is, it is done with the bare minimum of liquid. Without the space to bubble around in, the integrity of the ingredients is maintained. I had a ragù in Sicily, served with the curiously named priest–strangler pasta, which had been cooked for so long it was almost dry; still, the fibres of coarsely ground meat were discernible in the gravy, as was the distant ghost of celery, finely diced.

11

ON ALMOST-FRYING

So much for celery and onions, now neatly diced and piled to one side of your chopping board; we only need some carrots to complete the holy trinity. You might think that a carrot is always a carrot, but the difference in flavour between a good carrot – perhaps one that has been stored in sand to concentrate its essential carrotness – and a bad one is really so pronounced, and the cost of even an excellent carrot so small, that it is worth getting the best you can find, especially if you are just using three or four diced finely in a stew. I wouldn't bother with those rainbow heritage carrots you see in bunches sometimes, or at least not for cooking with: the purple ones juice nicely, and of course you have the pleasure of telling anybody who will listen that carrots were only bred a uniform orange in tribute to William of that name, but the fact is, the white ones taste of parsnip and the rest just taste of carrot – an overpriced and underwhelming carrot. They are often quite small, too, which seems to me, in a vegetable, like wasted potential.

So, get some good large carrots and rejoice in their orangeness; then, having scrubbed but not peeled them, cut them as finely as you did the celery and onion. Older cookbooks sometimes tell you to split carrots, as if they were logs, and indeed they can be rather woody. With this in mind, having cut the whole into two shorter logs and placed each upright on its round end, cut the carrot into short planks and stack these on top of each other. Each stack can now be cut lengthways into strips and then across into little cubes, at which point, as they fall apart, you can add them to the pile of vegetables, which now has the potential to become almost any stew, braise or daube you care to name, but is, in this case, destined only to be a ragù, a rich rabbit ragù. Whatever you're planning to do with it, the initial cooking is always the same: we intend to heat the vegetables to the point at which they release their juices, and then to concentrate and slightly caramelize those juices. This procedure, which goes by the name of 'sweating', is often demanded in recipe books without further explanation, as if it was something we were born knowing; it is not, it's true, a complicated operation, but it is one that should be approached with precision and care – like everything in cooking, I suppose. This started, of course, with the neat knifework and the little dice, which will cook so evenly and so well; or rather, you could say, it started with the choice of vegetable in the shop or market, or the growing and the watering, the planting of the seed or the bulb, the breeding and the movement of species across continents and centuries... In any case, a lot of work has gone into your raw materials, so there's no sense in messing them up now.

Next, you have to choose your pan. I have always found the saying 'a bad workman blames his tools' deeply irritating; he might well do so, but so does a good workman with bad tools. The point, I suppose, is that part of being a good workperson is choosing the correct tools. You couldn't have chopped those vegetables well without a good sharp knife, and you can't cook a stew properly without a good heavy pan. A chef I used to work with once told me that every piece of kitchen equipment should be capable, if it came down to it, of being used as a murder weapon; this might be putting it a bit strongly, but a good stewpot should certainly be sturdy enough to knock someone out. It needs to be heavy enough and made of a good enough metal, or other material, to achieve and retain a strong, even heat – the flame heating the pan, and the pan heating the food, not directly scorching it through thin, buckling metal. Cast-iron is excellent, of course, though if anything it is too heavy and does require a fair amount of care and attention. At home I have a sort of black, earthenware goblin-pot, which is quite effective, but at work we just use good-quality, thick-bottomed stainless steel. Non-stick saucepans, to my mind, have absolutely no reason to exist. If you think you are likely to let the bottom of a stew catch and burn, then you are quite likely also to forget not to use metal or detergent on the pan, or any of the other things you can do to destroy a non-stick coating and get bits of it in your food.

Just as important as weight is the size of your pan – relative to the things you intend to put in it, I mean. I would go so far as to say that it is impossible, in fact, to sweat vegetables properly in an inappropriately sized pan: too wide and they will have too much space and begin to colour and then singe before they are cooked; too small and they will steam more than sweat, and will also take far too long. On top of this, of course, you need to be able to fit in the rest of your ingredients. Ideally your soffritto should cover the thick base of your pan to a depth of around an inch, which allows you to use quite a lot of oil and to keep it at a fairly high heat, with frequent stirring and the judicious use of salt to avoid burning. Salt! It amazes me that this step isn't written into every cookbook in the world. Salt, you realize, helps to draw out juices from the vegetables, in which they can then cook; exactly, you'll recall, what we are trying to do. As they sweat, listen to them sizzling, the sound of extracted water interacting with hot oil; smell the different aromas of each as it rises; watch them, of course, as they turn translucent and then a light gold, and start, just start, to homogenize.

The words *soffritto* and *sofrito*, it seems, translate as 'almost fried' (as opposed to *refrito*, very fried, which we have mistranslated in refried beans), a description that refers both to the gentle sizzle of its cooking, not quite at the full fry of a fritter, and the length. As your ragù has a long stint in the pan to come, the vegetables do not, initially, need to have the life cooked out of them. This is different, you'll note, from the long cooking of onions alone. The important thing to remember in either case is that the way they are cooking initially, in a sweet glaze of oil or butter and their own juices, will end as soon as you add more liquid, whether stock or wine or water; from then on they will boil or rather simmer, and the flavour they have at that point is the flavour that will boil out of them and into your soup or stew, which is why we go through the different stages of stewing or braising and don't just throw everything into a pan.

In any case, we are getting ahead of ourselves again. Although it is perfectly possible to pre-chop your soffritto and put it in the freezer, or to pre-cook it and keep it in the fridge, we aren't that pressed for time. Our almost-frying will, in fact, come later, as we start to complete our meal. All we need to consider now is that water, and other mediums that are mostly water, cook ingredients differently from anything else. This is partly because water is wet, but mainly because of the temperature it is capable of reaching. Fresh water, at sea level or thereabouts, boils at 100 degrees centigrade, as I'm sure you are aware. What this means from a culinary point of view is that it is incapable of getting hotter than 100 degrees centigrade, and therefore so are things surrounded by it. The reason we place things such as delicate egg custards into a water bath when we bake them is not because we want the steam to keep them moist; it is because we do not want them to become hotter than water can get them. In the case of egg custards, in fact, we don't want them to become even that hot, and they will still overcook if left too long; the water just gives us a little more leeway.

There is a whole genre of recipe-writing centred around dishes you can leave quietly to themselves in the oven, or on the back of the stove; in go the ingredients, on goes the lid, and the human intervention with the meal is over, bar the eating. Convenience is a fine thing, of course, and I know that the goal is to remove the stress and the worry from cooking, but it has the exact opposite effect on me. I get anxious when I cannot keep a weather eye on the processes my ingredients are going through, as they heat or cool or dry or ferment. If I can't watch a collation of brassicas and alliums through the walls of their jar as the brine sours and clouds over, how am I supposed to know when they are ready? I don't have enough faith in time alone to tell me, so I keep my jars on the shelf, the better to get to know them through the warmth and the cold. If I am cooking a piece of fish or perhaps a whole one, I'll do it in clear liquid or on open fire. I admire the magic tricks of cooking *en papillote*, in clay or under salt, but I don't think they are for me. If there is a mixture of onion, carrot and celery making its steady way from raw to almost-fried in a good heavy pan, I will let them do so lidless and fill the kitchen with their steam; from time to time I will have a poke around, ostensibly to stir, but really just to see how everything is getting on. It's not strictly necessary, of course; I know, because of the size of my pan, the precise chopping of my vegetables, the salt and the oil I have added, that my soffritto is cooking gently in an emulsion of sweet juices and bitter oil, incapable, for the time being, of getting hot enough to burn. I still do it, though. The steady appreciation of constant change is one reason to cook.

12

ON SEASONING WITH SALT AND FAT

The beginning, the middle and the end; these are our three opportunities to salt – and indeed to add seasoning or flavouring of any kind to our food – and in my opinion far too much attention is paid to the beginning and end and not enough to the middle. Yes, the preparation, pre-salting or curing is vital, and the final adjustments make the flavours sing, but it's the stuff in the middle, the stuff that cannot, once the moment has passed, easily be done or undone, that is really the making of a dish. Think of the salt you add to keep the onions from burning, the salt you add to a loaf of bread, which, deadly to yeast, is what stops a good rise becoming a fall. If you cook pasta without salt in the water, you will never get enough flavour into it, no matter how many anchovies, olives or capers you add to its sauce; and there is no point in drowning a boiled potato in butter if you didn't salt it properly in the first place. Salt, in other words, is not just an add-on but something that needs fully integrating into your food, and without which everything may as well be ashes in your mouth – starches, perhaps, most obviously so.

Potatoes are delicious, or at least they are capable of being so. The problem is that, firstly, they need salt to become delicious, and secondly, their deliciousness is easily lost to boiling water; this is why chips are so much tastier than boiled potatoes, and why the potatoes in a Spanish tortilla should be cooked with the onions in oil. Their flavour is doubled, in that they possess the particular quality of umami, which, usually glossed over as simply a strong savoury flavour, refers in fact to ingredients that act specifically as a flavour enhancer for protein, a sort of single-purpose salt; this is why potatoes go so well with meat, with eggs and with beans and cheese. The seemingly bland one enhances the apparently stronger other. The most obvious way, then, to preserve the natural goodness (by which I mean the deliciousness) of potatoes is to cook them not-in-water; generally this means either in fat or in hot air. Chips, as I said, are the clearest example of this, but of course a large amount of their flavour is due to the fat you cook them in – preferably a well-clarified beef dripping. This is not a bad thing, but it does mean that you lose the simple purity of the potato. A baked potato would be perfect if you could also manage to season it to the core; you could, it occurs to me, brine it first, refrigerated so it doesn't start to ferment, before drying off and baking. I have never tried this, though, and anyway, baked potatoes take enough forward planning as it is. It is a shame that something so well suited to a quick and lazy meal takes some hours in the oven, but then I suppose that is what microwaves are for. Baked potatoes, of course, become, in time, the best mashed potato, at which point you can season as much as you like, but since the introduction of other flavours, usually butter and cream, but perhaps olive oil, garlic, lemon and almond, is almost the point of mashed potato, that's not quite relevant to our purposes.

No; the best way, to my mind, to get a potato that tastes perfectly of potato is to season it in the very middle of cooking, so the one operation is a part of the other. To boil it in such a way that everything lost to the water is reabsorbed in the cooking process; in other words, to carefully boil it dry, as we do most notably with rice, another seemingly bland starch with hidden depths. To do this, you want small potatoes that you would normally cook and indeed eat whole; ideally, you want particularly good ones, though it does seem to be a general fact that small vegetables taste more of themselves than larger ones. It is almost as if there is only a certain amount of flavour within each plant, and in the process of growing that flavour is spread thinner and diluted further. This could be just my imagination, but it certainly seems to hold true with potatoes. The smaller the better then, especially in the early spring when, if you'll recall, this meal is taking place and the first new-season crop of tiny, muddy potatoes appears – the first Jersey Royals, hopefully, though there are always good potatoes to be had – Pink Fir, Charlotte, Ratte, or whatever. They are almost always moderately local, if only because they are so heavy that the cost of their freight would outweigh any savings accrued by mass farming in Holland or Spain. As with carrots, potatoes are so cheap that even good ones are really not that expensive, unless you are making vats of mash, or Irish stew or a roast dinner for dozens; to accompany a little grilled fish at an early spring lunch, where people always eat fewer potatoes than you think they will and you are going to treat the ones you have with the utmost care, it is definitely worth getting the good ones, the ones you have to scrub clean.

When you have done so, put them in a pan or two so they fill it or them in a single layer; the quality of your pan is less important here, but size is still paramount. This is the kind of thing you want to eat lukewarm, and it has a much quicker cooking time than you might expect, so you can cook your potatoes in batches. Sprinkle a fair amount of salt, a hefty tablespoon of fine sea salt, into the pan, then add just enough cold water to cover the potatoes and place the pan over a high heat, bringing the water up to a fast boil where it will stay as you boil the pan dry. This can be a slightly unnerving operation, especially if you are on washing-up as well as cooking duty, because it feels you are going to ruin both potato and pan, but it works, and whatever residue is left is mainly salt and will dissolve away again. The water will bubble up around the potatoes, both steaming and boiling them, until it seems there is no moisture left; shake the pan, and you will see that there is. Carry on cooking and shaking until no wetness appears, and all of a sudden there is a sizzle and a thin layer of salt over everything, vegetable and metal. Tip the potatoes into a bowl and, if necessary, rinse out the pan to begin again. The results will look like tiny little jacket potatoes, and taste quite astonishingly of themselves – such is the gift of salt, which in this particular case grants more than just flavour. Salt water boils, you see, at a higher temperature than plain; not much higher, but enough for the skins to crackle and to crisp, as if from fire.

As a fairly straightforward enhancer of flavour, salt is the most obvious form of seasoning, and when recipes instruct you to check the seasoning, they normally mean that you should see whether there is enough salt in the dish; they often expect you to add pepper at this point as well, but that, in my opinion, is a spice not a seasoning, especially black pepper with its aggressive fruitiness. I'll add it routinely – as a spice – to egg- and dairy-based things, but that's about it. The rich blandness of something like a béchamel, or yoghurt or sour cream, well seasoned with salt and spiced with coarsely ground black pepper, should not be under-estimated – but that's by the bye. Seasoning, to my mind, is the full adjustment of the entire spectrum of tastes, by which we mean, of course, the simple flavours that we sense with our tongue; simple, that is, in the sense of base, vital. We grew up, or at least I did, with that map of the tongue with salt, sweet, sour and bitter laid out upon it, to which we now add umami, as everybody knows; more recent research indicates that we have dedicated tastebuds for fat, too. Some would add to this list various substances that have a marked physical effect on our tongue, for example the heat of chilli, the cooling sensation of mint and its relatives, the puckering dryness of tannins, though since they have similar effects if applied elsewhere on our bodies, I'm not sure they count as tastes as such, any more than actual heat and cold; at any rate, they don't fit into the theory of seasoning I am attempting to construct, so I'm going to ignore them here.

Think about a salad dressing. A salad, at least a lettuce salad, is all seasoning, and is defined by its dressing more than anything else; croutons and cos in a vinaigrette, for example, are not a Caesar salad, though they are still good to eat. The dressing does most of the work, and it can do that because it contains all of the basic tastes. Oil and vinegar, of course, are the key components, so straight off you have bitter, fat and sour, to which you add salt, a good amount of salt to offset that sourness, and, if you aren't using a particularly good vinegar, a pinch of sugar to make up the missing sweetness.

That just leaves umami, which is why so many salad dressings contain anchovy, capers, fish sauce, Worcestershire sauce, grated or mashed cheese, egg yolk or something of the sort. Salad dressing, especially a simple vinaigrette or lemon juice equivalent, is one of those things that is often thrown together at the last minute – which can be the best way to make it if it means that you are thinking on your feet and tasting as you go. You should do this with everything, of course, but salad dressing is a good place to practise, as it is quick to make and edible at every stage of its short making.

You start with the vinegar, which will decide the colour and the overall flavour of the whole thing; you taste it to see how sweet and sour it naturally is, which will decide everything else you do. Seasoning, really, is a matter of balance – of getting everything to the correct, balanced strength, so no one voice can be made out in the clamour. Vinegar, of course, is too sour to dress salad on its own, but rather than choosing something milder you add salt, dissolving it directly into the vinegar, as salt brings out the sweetness; you add oil, a good bitter olive oil, as bitterness balances sourness and fat calms them both. Tahini, for example, sesame seed butter, is something that I find unpalatably bitter, as well as too cloying to eat straight, but stir enough lemon juice and salt into it and the three strengths end up as something quite subtle, elusively so. It is possible that if you brined a lemon and ate it whole then the bitterness of the rind and the sourness of the juice would interact to create a delicious whole; I can't say that I have ever tried that, but I suppose that is essentially what a preserved lemon is, and I'll happily eat them whole and unadorned.

The same principle of balance applies even with something

apparently plain and one-dimensional, like a rich, meaty braise or ragù, which, in fact, to be successful and to completely fill the mouth with its flavour, needs just as neat a balance as a perky salad. In an odd sort of misdirection, the thing you spend the most time over – that neatly chopped and long-sweated soffritto – mainly seems to add sweetness to this savoury dish, at least in terms of essential tastes, although some alchemy of onion and celery also adds its own depths. Salt, of course, is added at every stage of cooking, with the depth of umami coming chiefly, if almost incidentally, from the meat itself, browned or otherwise; the possibility of anchovies, tucked into the melting vegetables, should not, however, be ignored. Bitterness is introduced with beer or wine, or even tea (especially if you are doing something involving spice and game and prunes), added directly to the soffritto and bubbled away to almost nothing before nestling the meat inside. Great handfuls of bitter herbs and greens added at the end do their job as well. I add vinegar to almost everything, but especially to stews and ragùs where I tend to use it twice, the first time almost at the beginning, with or before or just after the wine, or to scrub the most delicious bits from the base of the browning meat pan; the second time much later, when the bite of almost-raw vinegar brings definition to flavours flattened by the long cooking. The difference a long splash of sherry vinegar makes to a pan of collapsing oxtail is really astounding.

Fat? There are ten thousand ways of adding fat to a stew – or at least, say, three: at the beginning, the middle or the end. You cook the soffritto in fat, of course, or it wouldn't be fritto; whether you use clarified or whole butter, olive or sunflower or vegetable oil, lard or beef dripping or the rendered fat of fat-tailed sheep is largely a matter of personal preference, culture and religion. Each fat also carries its own secondary taste – milky sweetness or cultured sourness, the bitterness of seeds, a slightly rank meaty quality – which insinuates its way into the meal. Then you have the fat of your meat, unless you are stewing a wild animal, some rabbit perhaps, which have almost none of their own; in this case you might add diced bacon or perhaps a particularly fatty broth to provide that dense, tongue-coating richness. Then, of course, we might finish the whole thing with a last splash of olive oil, a dollop of aioli or sour cream. I can't quite think of the British equivalent, if there is one, but the Turkish habit of frying spices or dried herbs in sizzling butter and pouring the lot over meat, vegetables, pasta, or anything at all, is well worth borrowing, though in time you do come to wonder how you ever ate anything not covered in melted fat.

Any dedicated cook or eater will have heaved a profound sigh of relief at the rehabilitation of fat by recent research. Freed from the twin shackles of heart disease and obesity, dignified with its own particular place on our tongue, we now know that not only does fat 'carry flavour', as they say, but it is flavour in and of itself. I've never been entirely sure what that truism is intended to imply; perhaps that some things, to state it another way, have flavours and colours that are mainly or only soluble in fat; there are many spices, for example, which, if added ground to a pickling liquor or stock, would float upon it like pondweed but would sink willingly into sizzling butter – dried peppers in their various forms, most obviously. Just a pinch of paprika or those mild Turkish chilli flakes will dye quite a lot of fat a deep and vivid orange, while the heat in stronger ones, of course, dissolves just as effectively; that's why we drink fatty drinks to cool our mouths and why an ayran is a much better accompaniment to a kebab – or a lassi to a curry – than is a too-cold beer.

Many of the more demanding sauces of the French kitchen have fallen a little out of favour now; the various classical preparations of steak, for example, have mainly given way to iterations of mayonnaise and compound butter. This is undeniably a good thing, at least for anyone who really wants to taste the quality of their ingredient. A good steak, properly cooked, should barely need saucing, but herbed or spiced butter, pounded and chilled then melted over the meat, is hard to turn down. I have a particular soft spot for the so-called Café de Paris butter, which alongside the fat might contain anchovies, chopped cornichons or capers or shallots and a little paprika, and so is in itself a fairly complete seasoning. I also occasionally make a sauce of butter and seaweed, which contributes its own peculiar umami to a dish. What the fat does in dishes such as this, and I suppose what is meant when we say it carries flavour, is to provide a solid background against which to appreciate flavours and aromas which are themselves vagrant, fleeting and hard to pin down; if you eat a piece of seaweed, for example, there is a lot of salt, a passing whiff of the sea, and then it is gone. The butter brings it into sharp relief. The variety of old-fashioned herbs traditionally beloved of the British kitchen are also best captured in solid fat. Try celery, chervil, lovage especially, sorrel, caraway, ground elder, more Alexanders; just pick one, though, the better to appreciate it. Take a handful of lovage then, which is almost too strong to use in most applications; the special quality of fat is that you can stretch just a few leaves, nicely chopped, through a whole block of butter. Do it forcefully, in a food processor or a stand mixer or with a sternly wielded wooden spoon, to push the oils and the flavours out of the leaves and into the fat, and when the whole is one green with a few flecks of leaf, you can roll it up in baking parchment and keep it in the freezer, to take off slices as you need, as even frozen butter doesn't take long to melt over a resting hanger steak or a little flatfish straight off the grill; but first you'll want to dollop a spoonful over those slightly wrinkled little potatoes and enjoy, alongside the astringent, ancient taste of the herb, the good works of fat and of salt.

13

ON COOKING
WITH WINE
AND VINEGAR

Everyone knows that blood is thicker than water, but there is some
disagreement about the precise nature of wine. Something old and
rich, which reluctantly slides its way down the edges of a swirled
glass, can quite easily stain your teeth, your lips, your table and
indeed your shirt a dense red, as if you had in fact been feasting on
that life-giving forbidden fluid. On the other hand, the wine at the
last meal of Jesus of Nazareth, commemorated in the ritual during
which, apparently, the drink is turned literally into divine blood, is
likely to have been young, weak and further diluted with water. In
any case, far from the tannin and jam we are now expected to enjoy
with bloody meat, it would likely have been of a sourness most
modern drinkers would find distinctly unpalatable. Sourness, of
course, we find attractive in lemonade, pickles, ketchups, chutneys
and the like, but the particular vinegared sourness that emerges
in some wines, ciders, unusually fermented beers, and indeed in
vinegar can be off-putting, precisely because it is proximate to
decay – but this is only another way of saying that it is alive.

Most of the wine we drink, in common with much of the
food we consume, is a dead product, with deterioration and rot

its only possibilities for the future. The process of pasteurization, the brief super-heating which, destroying all microbial life, allows for longer storage of fruit juices, milk products, honey and the like, is a part also of the long interference that crushed grapes undergo on their journey into bottles. This includes the addition of farmed yeasts to replace the now-dead natural population, artificial preservatives and, in many cases, a forcible deconstruction of the wine into its constituent parts of alcohol, sugars, water, tannins and the like, in order to be reconstructed in a precisely calibrated fashion, which ensures a consistent and commercially viable end product. Now, there is nothing wrong with safety and consistency. Having access to more-or-less fresh milk without having to acquire it directly from the farm is something we all take for granted, as is the fact that we can go and buy a bottle of wine from the supermarket or the cornershop and know that it will taste exactly the same as it did yesterday, or last week, or probably will next year – which is the problem. For all that wine-makers like to talk about the particular terroir of their vineyards and the effect of the vagaries of weather on each year's particular vintage, the fact is that most of the artificial wines they sell, made with non-native yeasts, their edges blunted with preservatives, are made not as an expression of a particular grape or year but rather in a spirit of industrious commercialism.

If you taste a wine from one of the newer generation of makers, who uses older, indigenous varieties of grape, who ferments, as we did with our pickles, using the bacteria and yeast already swarming over their fruit, and who adds little or no extra material to preserve his finished product in the bottle, the effect can be quite astonishing. Such wines are often, if not always, a little sour, as they would have been at that last supper – as I say, although this is a comparatively recent trend amongst winemakers, the methods they use are ancient – but they are so as part of a more general breadth of flavour, with the extremes still in place, which I think justifies the effort and the expense of seeking them out. It's not that they're more expensive than artificial wines as such, but rather that no-one makes the very cheapest kind, which are in any case barely worth the money and certainly not suitable for a more or less celebratory lunch to be shared with friends. If you're going to drink at lunch-time, you may as well drink something good.

A lunch wine, of course, should be light; light enough firstly that it doesn't require you to take a nap after two or three glasses, and secondly that it will sit reasonably with everything you intend to eat. While I greatly admire the regimented procession of drinks in various food cultures, from clear aperitifs through darkening wines and into dense brandies and liqueurs, I think dinner is really the place for them. Sticking to one wine at lunch is probably best, even if you have several bottles of it. A pale, chillable red, with the tart notes of unripe berries, would be excellent, although for some people the stigma of rosé is too much to bear; in this case, I find prosecco is always appropriate, especially if you can get hold of the so-called *colfondo* type, unfiltered, of a biscuity dryness, and only gently sparkling; fizzy enough that drinking it feels like a cele-bration, but serious enough to accompany you through lunch and beyond – if, that is, you have any left over.

Taste a glass of wine that has been exposed to the air and its multitudes of bacteria for too long and you will taste the possibility of rot, lurking at the edges of your tongue; once you know that the potential is there and which particular threads of flavour lead off towards decay, it can be hard to untaste them even in perfectly good wine. The trick, I suppose, is to learn to enjoy it, however counterintuitive this may seem.

Brewing and vinification of any kind, involving as they do the breakdown and transformation of ripe organic matter by teeming micro-organisms into an often pleasantly psychoactive poison, are really, as with lactofermentation, a process of controlled rot. It is simply one whose products we have learned, both culturally and personally, to enjoy. If we could remember – really physically recall – the revulsion that most of us must have felt on first tasting the most innocuous of wines or beers, and the sheer bloody-mindedness with which we went through mixed drinks, sweet wines, fizzy ciders and cheap lagers to finally arrive at the point where we could honestly enjoy a glass of tannic red, a pint of stout or a Martini, then surely we would be more open to sour beers, orange wines, clouded ciders and medicinal Italian bitters. If, that is, we as a species had the ability to properly bring to mind sensations of pain and disgust, the way we can with guilt and pleasure, then we would not have to re-learn these things again and again as we drift slowly through adulthood. That's how it seems to me, anyhow, and so I make a point not to dismiss as inedible anything which is clearly not so, whether a product of age, bacteria, visceral animality or simply high modern processing. If there is something other humans enjoy which you do not, then that is merely because there is an area of your palate you have not yet reached; make the effort to acquire the taste or not, as you wish, but don't attack others for your own incompleteness. A taste that is refined in the sense of narrow is nothing to be proud of.

For example, until recently I had never encountered a bowl of tripe that I truly enjoyed; I found the texture challenging at best, the taste close to non-existent, the appearance – especially of the sort that looks like the ancient rug you keep for your dog – that of something you would not wish to ingest. I knew, of course, that cooks and eaters I respect loved the stuff, that the strange whitened mass lies at the heart of Neapolitan and Roman cuisine, the cooking of provincial France and Turkey and all over the world, but I could never find it in me to enjoy it. Still I persevered, and recently, on a brief trip to Spain, I had, perched on a table in the street in the full glare of the winter sun, a bowl of tripe stew, muddy and rich with chickpeas, blood sausage and paprika, and it was delicious – the tripe, finally, subdued into unctuousness, densely spiced by its companions in the long, slow simmer. The garnish of vinegar-sharp pickled chillies helped, I'm sure, providing a fresh beam through that meaty fug – though perhaps fresh is the wrong word to use, vinegar, of course, being doubly decayed.

The word vinegar itself simply means rotten wine, which is broadly accurate, at least for wine vinegar. It used to be thought that standing wine, exposed to the air, was turned sour by vinegar flies, or perhaps that these tiny insects bred in or were spontaneously spawned by standing wine. Leave a bowl of vinegar uncovered for an hour or two, especially in the summer, and you will see why this belief persisted, as dozens of flies you never knew were there will mysteriously suicide within it; I have no idea why they do this. We now know, of course, that wine, cider, mead, beer, and indeed any other kind of sufficiently weak alcohol, is soured, when exposed to the air, by the largely helpful acetobacter, which, as far as I understand the matter, consumes alcohol and excretes in its place acetic acid, much as yeasts were allowed to consume sugar in exchange for that same alcohol in the first place. As with lactobacteria and indeed yeasts, the acetobacter are everywhere, invisibly present, and in most cases, given the right environment, it is harder not to make vinegar than to do so; you just need to expose as much of the alcohol to the air as possible, though ideally with some covering to stop dust and of course flies from getting in.

If you find this a little haphazard – and it can take a surprisingly long time for a vinegar colony to establish itself – then you can jumpstart the process with one of those bottles of live cider vinegar you get in healthfood shops, which are usually advertised as containing probiotic cultures or else the vinegar mother, the unqualified word 'bacteria' still apparently anathema to marketing copywriters. Whereas lactobacteria and yeasts are visible only by the marks they leave upon their world, by the milky sourness and the bubbles of carbon dioxide, you can see a vinegar mother as a distinct entity, a strange cloud of alien matter floating within your bottle; there is something quite pleasing about this. Although there are, I'm sure, quicker ways to go about this, I have found it best to add your new wine only gradually to the live vinegar. The alcohol the acetobacter feed on will, in too high a concentration, swiftly overwhelm them; they can tolerate greater amounts than most bacteria, to be sure, which is why, like the acid-loving lactobacillus, they are so useful, but they are not invincible and too much too quickly will kill them. Begin, then, with a bottle of live vinegar and about an equal amount of your chosen alcohol, and pour them both into one of those drinks-dispenser jars with a tap near the bottom. What alcohol you use does of course depend on both your personal taste and what you think you might often have going spare. My vinegar culture at work is a repository for unfinished bottles of red wine, though I have also made a fairly successful one from sourdough beer; to be honest, though, that particular brew was perhaps halfway towards vinegar anyway. Whatever you choose, leave it for a week or so to settle in and sour before you do anything else to it.

If you intend to use your vinegar for proper shelf-stable laying-up-for-the-winter pickling, then you should find some way of testing it for acidity for your own peace of mind; I've got a digital pH meter, but until recently I relied on those rolls of indicator paper you used at school, which should turn a pleasant orange, around three on the scale, when dipped into your vinegar. If, on the other hand, you only wish to use it for dressing, sauces, finishing ragùs and braises, and so on, you can go by taste. It should, of course, taste like vinegar, though do bear in mind that just because it is homemade does not necessarily mean it is very good; most decent vinegars you can buy are aged somewhat, for one thing.

Anyway, when you are happy that your wine has rotted, then you can double it with alcohol and leave again to sour so you end up with four times as much vinegar as you started with. Draw off what you want through the tap, and replace the amount you have taken with more wine; keep this rhythm going and you will never have to buy vinegar again, although you will probably find that you start using it everywhere, little splashes here and there, bringing bursts of sweet and sour decay to your meals.

Although it is central to our particular traditions of chutneys, tracklements and sauces, and to the sharp pickles of chip shops and ploughman's lunches, I think vinegar is perversely under-rated in the British kitchen, to the detriment not only of our own cuisine but also of our understanding of those of other countries. The Sicilian dish *caponata*, for example, which sits somewhere between a stew and a relish, is often described as merely a heavily seasoned ratatouille, a sun-swollen celebration of aubergine and capsicum; really, though, it is a showcase for vinegar, and can be made with almost any vegetable — such as celery, as I mentioned before — although the other main ingredient is patience. There is a tendency, I find, as with other apparently simple preparations of vegetables, to rush the making of caponata, to cook the whole lot together into one homogenous slop, when really each element should be prepared separately, then combined and left at a warm room temperature, the flavours allowed to mingle and penetrate parts which remain physically distinct.

There are three parts to a caponata, as with most things: the sauce, the vegetable and (for want of a better word) the garnish. Dice two or three onions, those same sweet white ones, as finely as you can, and sweat slowly in good oli e oil along with a few cloves of plump garlic (and salt, of course), sliced thinly or crushed, until the whole begins to melt and combine. If this was a summer caponata, you would add tomatoes at this point, good ripe tomatoes cut into chunks, and let them collapse into a sauce, but since – as you'll remember – this is a spring meal, the onion will form the whole of the bulk, so pay the appropriate attention to its cooking. With this in mind, you can get together the rest of the ingredients, such as they are: honey and vinegar and perhaps a little dried chilli. How much of these things you use is really up to you, especially if you are cooking with that homemade wine vinegar of uncertain strength, but there should be a fair amount of vinegar, say a couple of hundred millilitres or a decent glassful, and then enough honey for the sweetness to balance out the acid. Again, if we were making a summer caponata with its jumble of different ingredients, the glowing amber notes of honey might seem a little too much, and simple white sugar would take its place, but at the end of a long winter and with only a few other ingredients to jostle against, a good honey, which needn't necessarily be set or runny or single-varietal, but should be good to eat on over-buttered toast, is just the thing. Use chilli if you want to add chilli, which you know better than me, and add the lot, sweet and sour and all, to the melting onions, letting the vinegar bubble and reduce for just a couple of minutes, to keep its raw edge.

So much for the sauce. The celery, which needs peeling if you think it needs peeling, should be cut into little squares about the size of a standard postage stamp, and then treated simply as if you were making almost any kind of meat stew, which is to say you should fry it in a hot pan, in batches and salting as you go, to ensure the chunks of vegetable brown rather than steam, removing each load with a slotted spoon when they are coloured all over, and adding a fresh splash of oil before the next batch goes in; it might seem strange to pay this much attention to a vegetable, but that is a simple matter of refocusing your brain a little or, to put it another way, reassessing your priorities. If you think, as many seem to, that animal protein tastes naturally more complex, more interesting, and essentially more delicious than any product of vegetable, fruit or fungus does, then it really makes sense to pay it less attention in the kitchen. If anything, it makes sense for the meat portion of your meal to be cooked either first, and allowed to braise on the back burner or in the oven, or last, seared over a fierce heat, while you devote the bulk of your time and concentration to the careful seasoning and cooking of supposedly bland vegetables.

That, at any rate, is what I tell myself when cooking pan after pan of neatly diced celery and scooping each load into the sauce waiting to one side off the heat but still warm. Two heads of celery take a surprisingly long time to cook in this way, and it is, I must admit, something of a relief when the process is complete and you can stir the sauce to dress each piece and put the whole lot to bed for the evening, or perhaps the morning, covered and left out of the fridge. A little time before lunch, or whenever you intend to eat your relish, you can begin to finish it off. It will definitely require a small handful of capers and the same of roughly chopped mint leaves, both of which go extremely well with celery and vinegar; it might also need a final adjustment of the levels of salt, sweetness and sour, all of which we experience differently when tasted at room temperature. Even if we had been using a commercially made vinegar, with its edges pasteurized out and its acidity and sweetness carefully regulated, its fresh kick when added cold is very different from the mellowness of its cooked taste, almost as different as it is from the bright tang of lemon juice, which might also be nice, added with a good pinch of sea salt left whole and coarse so you can feel the grains individually against your questing tongue.

I'm not entirely sure where all of this fits into our meal. Sometime before it really gets going, I suppose, caponata being well suited to the antipasto part of the meal, during which the Italians seem to consume most of their vegetables; it's just as suited, though, to eating alongside a little oily fish, perhaps with the skin still bubbling from the heat of the grill. I've read that caponata always used to contain fish, chunks of sardine or mackerel cooked in the sour sauce in a similar manner to *escabeche* or *sarde in saor*, and its replacement with aubergine or celery was due only to the increasing poverty of the Sicilians as a succession of invaders and exploiters took the stunning cornucopia of the island and turned it into wealth kept hidden or far away from its inhabitants; this doesn't seem entirely convincing to me. Although meat is scarcer in Sicily than it is in much of mainland Italy, and still seems to be associated with feast days, the islanders have no shortage of fish, especially oily ones, which they put in every conceivable place and preparation, stuffed like songbirds, tossed through pasta, melted into sauces, and as seasoning on pizzas and in denser breads; more likely, I think, is that caponata has always been a catch-all term for these sweet-and-sour preparations, whether of various vegetables or of seafood, and the fish variety has simply fallen out of fashion. People forget that the history of cuisine is influenced as much by the fickleness of taste as it is by the inexorable currents of history and economics – though where those tastes arise is another matter.

14

ON BOILING
FEET AND BONES

Some things, of course, are beyond the rise and fall of fashion, and
a look at the goodness, the rich thickness extracted in the long
boil of soup- or stock-making, is enough to know that bones are
one of them. It is easy to believe that bones, lying as they do in
the depths of ourselves, are the repository of the soul, or at least
of special, vitally animal instincts; we know things, as they say,
in our bones, that even the flickering lizard brain has forgotten.
Why do we venerate the broken bones of saints and of heroes?
Why do we decorate grand halls, pubs, hotels and museums with
those of deer, of rabbits and of dinosaurs? Practically, of course,
it is because they are that which does not rot; our one hope, as
fragile vertebrates, of immortality, beyond whatever ephemera we
leave behind on the earth. Certainly the bones of the animals we
use for food are the part of them that lasts the longest, and it is a
shame that, for most home cooks, they are the part least likely to be
seen, although fashion again seems to be turning against the neat,
boneless segments of meat, barely identifiable as animal, which
occupy the larger part of supermarket meat shelves and butchers'
counters. Every cook should be able to look at a carcass and, as

T.S. Eliot said of Webster, 'see the skull beneath the skin' – see it, weigh it, and begin gathering ingredients.

Last summer, in the course of making a rather fine pie, I took four pigs' heads and boiled them – really boiled them – with onions and carrots and all the usual accompaniments until the skin and flesh began to peel away from cartilage and tooth and bone, their plump, slightly smug faces dissolving into the water to reveal the lean, rangy skull; our fat Large Whites, long domesticated and bred for consistency, are still wild boar somewhere in their genes and in the bones beneath. As the flesh flaked off, first in chunks of skin and fat and then the nuggets of the cheeks and the surprisingly delicate tongue, I scooped out the chunks of meat, leaving the rest to boil for, as I remember, a day and a night. I was left with a milky elixir and, lurking resiliently in it, the bones. It has been common practice throughout the history of human civilization to make various outrageous claims as to the health benefits of the foods we eat, and indeed the techniques of cooking, of medicine and of magic have always been thoroughly intertwined. The great variety of dishes served at a grand Tudor banquet, for example, many of them of great culinary delicacy and skill, was as much to do with health as with conspicuous consumption. The then-current medical thinking required the four classical humours, the body's vital fluids, to be properly in balance for optimum physical and mental health, which could be achieved partly through diet; so, for example, a fit of melancholy, caused by an excess of black bile, which was associated with the classical element earth and therefore considered cold and dry, might be cured with food both hot and wet. It is hard, it's true, to feel melancholic while consuming tea, noodle soup or indeed pigs' head broth, but while it is attractive to believe there was a glimmer of truth in all such apparently primitive beliefs, we should remember that the theory of humourism forbade the eating of fresh fruit and vegetables for many a long year; in any case, all its practitioners are now dead.

Yet when you look at the mass of so-called diet books, which appear every January without fail on the lists of otherwise respect-able publishers, it is hard to believe that we have really progressed all that far since those days, when the king's stoical nature forbade him cucumber salad. Now, of course, with technical advances and far quicker dissemination of both knowledge and ignorance, we can see these fashions rise and fall as if in time-lapse, with trend followed by backlash followed by compromise or disappearance, all in fast and inevitable succession; this is certainly the case with bone broth, the subject of a great number of dubious claims. Now, the nutritional value of broth or really anything else is something that doesn't particularly interest me; that boiled bones contain protein and fat, calcium and gelatine seems obvious, but as I don't suggest you make them the cornerstone of your diet I don't see that it matters how much of these or other nutrients actually make their way into your body. Well-intentioned commentators, however, while rightly questioning woolly science and modern-day quackery, have, as it were, thrown the bones out with the bathwater; rushing to attack on all fronts, they deride bone broth, that supposed miracle substance, as nothing more than good meat stock. This is clearly not the case. Something like a *tonkotsu*, for example, or that pigs' head broth I made last summer, which was opaque, lip-sticking and buttery, is hardly comparable to even a ham stock, which is itself a very different thing to a well-made chicken stock – in ways besides the obvious. Stock is a background, while broth dominates; stock, we might say, is something that you do to water, while bone broth is most definitely something that you do to bones. To put it more concretely, stock is simmered and broth is boiled.

Now, while pigs' heads are generally cheap (mine were free), pans large enough to hold them and the time needed to cook them into total submission are not; in any case, the result is far too rich for a spring lunch. A subtler effect can be found a little closer to the ground, in the trotter. In my first kitchen job back in that small hotel, once a week, we used to get a delivery of great chunks of veal bones and a bagful of sawn-off pigs' feet, which would be fiercely roasted until dark brown and placed in a gigantic pot along with carrots, onions, leeks, celery, peppercorns, juniper, bay and rosemary. This would be filled with water and brought to a simmer, where it stayed, puttering away on one of the six burners, for at least four days, during which time it would have added to it mushroom trimmings, leftover roast tomatoes, almost any vegetable peelings aside from potato and, occasionally, eggshells, which I don't think had any place in there. It was my job, more often than not, to lift the huge pan from the back of the stove and down on to the floor. From this slightly more convenient position the broth would be scooped out and pushed through a large conical sieve into a clean pan, covered and heaved downstairs to the cellar, to be brought up again the next day for further simmering and reduction, then more sieving, mixing with wine and redcurrant jelly, and a final reduction by half to create a rich demi-glace, gelatinous enough, thanks to the trotters, to be solid when cold. This dense substance, re-melted into gravy, was almost exclusively used to moisten the potatoes and pre-sliced meats for the Sunday crowd – who would probably have preferred Bisto. A vegetarian at the time, it is fair to say that I did not entirely appreciate this process. It is only in the last couple of years, in fact, that I have really come to understand the virtues of a well-made stock.

The veal demi-glace, tasting as it does of a universal, primal meat, dark and heavily reduced by vicious boiling, is rather less popular than it once was, and as with many things, the number of ingredients and the cooking time of stocks has decreased, allowing the meats, mushrooms or vegetables involved to taste more cleanly of themselves. If you made a stock, say, from the crushed shells of crustaceans or from the bones or cartilage of flat or other white fish, you would let it sit at the very gentlest of murmurs, with perhaps only one bubble at a time lazily breaking the surface, for just fifteen or twenty minutes. The vegetables, in this case probably onion and fennel, celery and the white parts of leeks, should be diced correspondingly finely, rather as we do for a soffritto; the fat chunks of vegetable suitable to a meat broth would barely even cook through in such a short time. If you were very organized, you might make the vegetable stock first, boiling larger pieces of vegetable with perhaps some fennel seed, peppercorns and lemon peel to make sure it was strongly and cleanly aromatic, before slipping in the fish bones or pounded crab shells and letting them transform the whole; we aren't making fish stock, though. I've never had much occasion to make fish stock at home anyway. Either you buy whole fish and cook them whole, or you buy fillets.

Chicken stock is, for some reason, considered or at least treated as neutrally savoury, lacking the aggressive meatiness you get from dark beef bones or the distinctive traits of the animal that come out when boiling lamb or goat, and bringing, if made properly, a delicate golden colour as well as a subtle thickness and a certain gelatinous density to whatever you are cooking. A white risotto made with chicken stock, vermouth and good butter and cheese is about as perfect as plain food can get, up there with a cauliflower cheese or bread sauce; as it's not considered acceptable to eat bread sauce by the bowlful, risotto wins out. Still, I think even chicken stock has its limitations and doesn't in fact need to find its way into every savoury dish in the kitchen. Some rice dishes are better off made with water, though not so much for flavour's sake as for texture's; in a pilaf, for example, where you want each grain to stand dry and separate from its colleagues, that lip-smacking density combined with the natural starches in the rice can lead to a certain gluiness, however well you steam it and however well you fork it apart. Perhaps because of the popularity of stock cubes, bouillon powders and those little pots of jelly, people seem to forget that stock is as much about the weight of its physical presence as its taste; this is especially the case when made from pigs' trotters.

The complicated structure of bone and tendon that is a pig's foot, with its oddly dainty toes, the pinkly human cast of its skin and that funny, almost-opposable little back claw, has, we're told, a great deal to do with the famous intelligence of the pig, probably the cleverest animal – apart from the terrifying octopus – commonly eaten by humanity across large stretches of the world. Although pigs in this country are generally fairly well treated, at least by comparison with chickens and cattle, in the rest of Europe, across Asia and particularly in the USA, they are kept in conditions of torture and confinement which their intelligence chafes against and yet often learns to exploit. It is, for example, quite common to equip intensively farmed pigs with collars armed with remote sensors giving them access to one portion of food per mealtime, a neat system requiring little human intervention. The swine, however, realizing that their meals are apportioned not by divine providence but by virtue of the collar, will gather ones dropped or wrest them from fallen comrades so as to collect for themselves an extra portion, thus growing fatter and therefore hastening their own inevitable demise.

Perhaps, then, that is not the best example of the intelligence of pigs, but I doubt I would do any better under such extreme conditions. Left to their own happier devices, pigs show themselves better, involved in complex social interactions, capable of reasoning, recognition, and even of scheming against and manipulating their fellow swine; there is a reasonably compelling argument to be made that pigs have domesticated us as much as we have them, accepting certain sacrifices in return for warmth, food and shelter. If left under-fed, in fact, pigs will start almost immediately to regress back to wild boar-hood, even within a single generation. Starve a piglet and its snout and legs will lengthen as it readies itself for escape and the rigours of the wild; it will grow cunning and lean, exposing the intelligence that its forebears hid behind those floppy ears – and all of this, apparently, can be traced back to the trotter. Although goats, I suppose, have a certain belligerent wile, neither deer nor sheep are particularly noted for their intelligence and this is partly down to their clumsy hooves. The pig, with that funny little back claw, can almost grasp things, and can certainly drag them closer to hold in view, or rather, in place for snuffling at, for smelling, feeling and remembering. Whether we learn to remember because we have things to hold or we learn to hold so we have something to remember is a moot point, I suppose, but what is certain is that a trotter is dextrous, unusually so for a hooved foot, and is therefore composed, apart from nail and fat and skin, of a great quantity of sinew and tendon, wrapped around those solid bones.

We say that stock is made of bone, but it is really these connective tissues we are after, along with the fat, as it is these that break down into clouds of sticky gelatine when subjected to a long and persistent boil, creating a liquid thick and gentle enough to nurture the most delicate of meats, even something as essentially fat-free as hare or rabbit, through the long cooking that such hard-worked flesh requires. A few trotters go a long way, and four will make plenty of the kind of broth so dense it jellifies almost at room temperature; since we aren't using the flesh for anything in particular, you don't even have to shave them, which is usually the oddest part about using these cheap, under-valued pieces of animal. They do need blanching, though, as you'll see when you're doing it; once you have covered them in cold water and brought it to a vigorous boil, a sort of greyish-green scum will begin to ooze out of the feet. Not the most pleasant sentence to read in relation to cooking, I know, but you should let it happen, skimming off anything solid enough to collect on the surface, for about ten minutes, and reassure yourself that at least none of this is making its way into your stock. Once they are thoroughly blanched, drain the lot, give the trotters a rinse, and return them to the washed pan with a couple of onions, sticks of celery, a carrot or two and perhaps a leek, all cut into pretty careless chunks. Cover with fresh water, bring to a simmer and leave there for hours, letting the knuckle jack-knife and clench as the tendons give way and the skin contracts and punctures, until there is nothing left in the dense liquor but unidentifiable vegetables and bones.

15

ON COOKING
FLESH

I occasionally think that if I were devising a course of study for aspiring cooks, I would have them start at the beginning of life on land (the sea would be a different, deeper course) with preparations of vegetables and fungus, yeasts and bacteria; moving on to the animal kingdom, they would start with the eggs of birds, perhaps comparing them with those of lizards or fish, and move on to blood, then organ meat, then the lesser-used appendages and muscles. Only after years of patient work in the mastery of protein, carbohydrate, fat and heat would they be allowed to know the simple joy of cooking a pork chop or a steak, crisping a skin-on chicken breast or grilling a butterflied leg of lamb to a perfect blush. I did this myself in a way, entirely accidentally; I ate almost no meat for ten years, exactly when I was learning to cook, and so I'd like to think I got to grips with vegetables thoroughly, learning when to sear, really sear and burn them, when to boil, to leave them raw, to dress, to leave plain and so on. It is harder, to my mind, to cook vegetables than it is to cook meat, or at least to make them delicious, and it is not just a lack of interest or effort that leads to the paucity of vegetable cooking still often found here; it is just not something that enough people learn.

Through this, and then through working largely with the cheaper pieces of meat (bellies, shoulders, knuckles, and the like), I learned to pay attention to what I was cooking, which is all that anyone means when they say something is difficult to cook – that you have to pay attention the whole way through. Fried eggs, for example, are quite difficult to get just-so and, unless you know your pan and your stove very well, require near-constant care, basting and shuggling around and so on; as they are normally something cooked only in small amounts and for personal consumption, most people don't notice this. Take bacon, on the other hand, especially streaky bacon; all you have to do is put it on a tray and put that under the grill or in the oven, and your nose should do the rest. The best way to cook it is to do nothing to it, not even look at it – which seems to slow the process – until it is cooked. This is why breakfast works so well as a home-cooked meal: you cook the eggs, but the bacon cooks itself.

That is an extreme example, I suppose, and bacon is not an expensive or prime cut of meat as such; it is, rather, the value added by the curing and drying process that makes it so. Take, then, a chicken breast, a good one, mind, from a free-range, slow-grown organic bird, well muscled and plump, with at least a little fat between the skin and the meat – a rightly expensive piece of flesh. You could do a number of things to it, of course, depending on how crisp you want the skin, how moist you want the flesh, how long you have before dinner is required, and, of course, your own or your guests' tastes, and what you intend to serve with it; or you could just put it in the oven, quite a hot oven, for about ten or fifteen or twenty minutes. Really, though, there are so many variables – the precise size of your breast and whether you brined it, kept it in the fridge or took it straight from the shopping bag and into the pan; what kind of pan you put it in; what kind of oven you have and how well it works, as well as the actual temperature you set it to, since I didn't, in fact, specify – that it would be not only pointless but misleading and even dangerous to give you an exact time. You cook it until it is cooked, which you can ascertain by prodding or using a probe thermometer, or just by slicing a bit off and having a look; it should be white, and the muscle fibres should have begun to separate in a similar but finer way to those of fish, and if it isn't and they haven't, you can put the lot back into the oven and leave it there until it is and they have without doing appreciable harm to the whole.

I say expensive cuts, but really the cheaper parts of chicken are just as simple to cook – or easier, if anything; being composed of juicier muscle, the legs are much more forgiving of forgetfulness on the part of the cook, and in fact respond extremely well to very slow cooking indeed. Chickens, though, are expensive birds, or at least they should be. A generation ago, to eat one was a rare treat and had to be weighed up against its corresponding value as a producer of eggs; you'd be more likely to eat a tough old boiler, her laying days long gone, than the forcibly grown adolescents which now line the shelves of supermarkets everywhere, their pale and flabby meat a sad testament to the accelerated misery of their short, dark lives. It is a terrible thing that affordable food for all has come at such a cost to the wider environment, to the animals themselves, and to the delicate balance that everywhere wavers between animal, medicine and disease. How to tell people, though, that they must only eat chicken if they are willing to spend five or more times as much on a free-range, organic slow-grown bird, that the cheapest ones are not really chicken in taste, in appearance or in life? In any case, the fact remains that even a battery chicken is easy to cook, if not to make particularly delicious, and that is not only because it is the way it is but because it is consistently so. The domesticated animals we eat, especially but not exclusively the more intensively farmed and therefore cheaper ones, will as a rule have been bred and fed according to a programme of scientific rigour and cold avarice. A farm is a business, where the minimum possible amount of food and time is invested in exchange for the maximum amount of meat; although free-range farming might allow for a degree of uncertainty, in general every chicken from a particular farm will have been fed the same thing at the same time for every single day of its short life and you could, if you wanted, calculate exactly what the contents of each animal's stomach was at any given moment.

If this is only the inevitable result of the impulse towards profit and efficiency as it spreads across all fields of human activity, even those most essential to life, then the homogenizing effect it has had on our cooking, the loss of instinct and skill, and the building in its place of complacency and even laziness is still hard to stomach.

To get back to our meal, once upon a time, which really was not that long ago, you had to know how old a rabbit was before you could begin to cook it. If you didn't know, you would have to work it out, feeling the size and the strength of the muscle, the development of the tendons in the legs, the various scars of a violent life, before you could decide what exactly was going to be for dinner. Of course we all know that the vast array of vegetables and fruit constantly at our disposal from supermarket, cornershop, and even from the more traditional greengrocer is a very modern luxury, the product of a global network of producers and distributors, which annihilates time and distance for the sake of convenience; the idea that even the centrepiece of our meal might be beyond our control, that we might eat whatever we could get, cooked as it needed to be cooked, seems to belong to a much older time, when the cooks huddled together in the warmth of cave or hut as they waited, ever-hopeful, for the hunters to come home.

This has, of course, been the case for the greater part of human history; it is likely, in fact, that the current era of consistency and convenience will come to be seen as a blip, a strange, decadent moment during which we lost the ability to properly look at and consider the ingredients we had to hand before we began to cook. It is easy to see how the decadence starts, though. The greater the consistency of our ingredients, the less we have to think about cooking them and the more we can do so by rote or simply from memory rather than by observation, and so the less we need to care or at least understand about the lives of these creatures that we choose to eat – and why should we be willing to put much effort into cooking something we don't care about? So it goes on, and we move further and further away from the point where we could simply look at a piece of meat, or perhaps even a whole unbutchered animal, and say how it might need to be cooked, in what medium, over what time and temperature, how the muscle will shrink, how many the flesh might feed...

To put it another way, we have, under the current system, no particular reason, or at least no incentive to think about the things we cook and the lives they lead before they end up splayed on our chopping boards, in our fruit bowls, or lurking semi-frozen at the back of our fridges. If the few notes I have collected here have any purpose beyond sharing a few thoughts on the planning and cooking of a simple spring meal, one to share perhaps with family or with close friends, then it is to offer such a reason, or perhaps to suggest – as an incentive – that we don't really need one, or at least, once we have started, we don't need a reason to carry on. Once you begin to look at such things more closely, it swiftly becomes its own reward, and to meander slowly around the complicated ancestry of a particular preparation of sardines, say, the convoluted journey that the chicken has taken on its way to being the most popular meat and the most populous bird in the world, or the secret lives of the common rabbit, seems the most natural thing.

16

ON THE LIVES
AND DEATHS
OF RABBITS

We like to think of rabbits as cute, sociable creatures, occupying the greenest and most picturesque of our landscapes, always more Beatrix Potter than *Watership Down*, though in reality they live lives of violent sexual and political intrigue belonging to much more adult fiction, with territorial struggles, incest and partner-swapping erupting occasionally into vicious, sometimes fatal combat, their lives shadowed always by the constant terror of human and other predation, as well as the grim shadow of myxomatosis. Think, for example, of that calm and happy scene of rabbits grazing in a summer twilight, spread across the grass beside their hidden burrows; in fact they are eating for their lives, desperately feeding as quickly as they can, consuming far more than they can digest while still in the bleak open sky, wishing only to return beneath the cold ground, where they will defecate their barely chewed feast back into their own mouths, to eat at their leisure. This, anyway, is the overriding impression you get from studies on the subject, such as R.M. Lockley's *The Private Life of the Rabbit*, a book I found quite by chance while looking through the cookery section of a local second-hand bookshop and straying naturally into the adjacent shelves. This deeply peculiar book, written purely as a tie-in to a BBC television series, combines the results of a scientific study on the eponymous subject with the frequently wayward musings of its author, who can never quite avoid the human tendency to anthropomorphism he so often wags his finger against. All the rabbits in his study are given names, for example, which, though I suppose he considered it necessary to maintain the clarity of his narrative, certainly has an emotional effect of its own.

Perhaps because of the populist nature of the book, Lockley makes little effort to maintain much in the way of a scientific detachment, and he expresses particular admiration for the rather medieval society of the rabbit: the closely maintained feudal system, centred on the king buck, with his queen, concubines, scheming retainers, subordinates, children and grandchildren occupying the warren around him, all of which can change hands as a result of bloody, biting duels. The research team, in fact, engineer such a dynastic challenge by physically removing the king from his court and replacing him only when a rival has taken his place. The rival, psychologically boosted by his new-found status, beats the old king, seeing him off with a particularly vicious bite to the base of the ears; throughout all this squabbling, the does, who seem to be really in charge, stay tending their homes and their families. The fight for dominance, in fact, seems often to be the fight for the best warren and the best queen.

Occasionally, when he turns his gaze away from these antics on and below the ground, Lockley's prose takes flight in a kind of apocalyptic secularism, which, perhaps understandable as the inevitable flipside to the atheistic Romanticism often found in nature-writing, is striking, almost jarring, in what is after all a scientific work designed as a TV tie-in. For example, having spent a chapter describing the process of resorption, whereby does under physical or psychological stress can fully absorb — without blood or abortion — their unborn kittens, exercising an unconscious birth control on populations unable to support much growth, he turns his attention to the same problem in humanity. If you'll bear with me, I'd like to repeat what he says in full; while not, it must be said, strictly relevant to the proper construction of a rabbit ragù, it seems increasingly so to the condition of the wider world and therefore, if only tangentially, to dinner. In any case, it is interesting, I think, to know the thoughts of someone who has spent so much time observing a creature that is to most of us only a distant sight — or perhaps an ingredient.

At present, Lockley writes, man continues to breed almost uncontrolled and, like the rabbits, is rapidly destroying his environment by building over the face of the land which is more than ever needed for the production of his food and for his recreational needs. He is destroying his heritage; he is heading for a crash and this may be triggered off, as in the rabbits, by mechanisms beyond his control, that is to say, beyond the control of the sane majority of men. That trigger is likely to be a nuclear one, pulled by some dictator or other madman whose endocrine glands, under territorial stress (fear mania), like those of the rabbit in the same situation, are suddenly deranged metabolically.

Man is unlike the rabbit in one respect; he does not live by bread alone. But if he continues by over-population to burrow into and destroy the countryside, killing out other forms of wildlife, laying waste with bricks and concrete the few beautiful places on earth where he can rest and recuperate from the foul exhaust of his cities, he will indeed soon come to live by bread alone. Up to the time of the final crash he will live in a synthetic burrow, feed on frozen and tinned supermarket produce and pills, drink some of his own excrement (already today his excrement is discharged into rivers which are pumped into reservoirs to supply his medicated drinking water) and become as automated as, and even more helpless to avert disaster than, the rabbit.

Having delivered himself of this rather terrifying sermon, Lockley returns, as if nothing much has happened, to the matter at hand, which was myxomatosis. It must have seemed, writing in the teeth of the Cold War, that he was describing a future which could at any moment become the present, that humanity had come almost to the end of its history and was every day on the brink of its final disaster. That's not to say, however, that the problems he described have in any sense been solved; only that, without the ever-present shadow of nuclear devastation hanging over our heads, they currently seem less urgent. If anything, though, they are even more so. I have a cookbook — in case you thought I had forgotten about cooking — called *Countryman's Cooking*, by W.M.W. Fowler, which has also, as you might expect, a great deal to say on the subject of the rabbit. Although published only seven years before Lockley's, the book seems to come from another era entirely, which in a sense it does; while Lockley was writing up the results of his experiments almost as they occurred, Fowler's work is an account and the culmination of over two decades of living and cooking in the countryside, stretching back to, and occasionally beyond, the years of the Second World War, during which he served as the pilot of a Lancaster bomber and spent several years in a prison camp.

Throughout most of his work, Fowler maintains the tone you might expect of a man of his era and class, living a life that was even then studiedly anachronistic, and writing a book that seems intended to be as much slightly eccentric memoir as it is practical handbook; witty, dry to the point of flippancy, and small-c-conservative, with everywhere the impression of a stiff upper lip crowned with a neatly trimmed moustache. Sometimes, though, he allows the pain and the anger, which you can imagine must have bubbled always under the well-kempt tweedy façade, to spill out and on to the page, just as a thickening tomato sauce bubbles fiercely under the surface waiting only for a good stir into the corners to let it break loose. Unsentimental, in general, about the sanctity of life – as people who live in the countryside tend to be – willing to talk of trapping and netting, shooting, skinning and gutting, he reserves a special horror for the disease myxomatosis; or rather, because he has no spare anger to waste on futility, for its concerted propagation across the wild rabbit population of Britain through a combination of direct action and deliberate inaction by the political and scientific authorities of the time. As a pilot, Fowler must have seen less of chemical warfare than many in the trenches, but he was certainly not untouched by it, at least if the absolute moral loathing he feels for those who would use such means against an innocent and wild population is anything to go by. As much as it was unsporting, inhumane and indeed inhuman, though, he seems to think that this particular cull, which after the few short years in which the disease was most virulent saw only one in one hundred rabbits left alive, was just plain stupid.

As Fowler has it, the rabbit warren, though originally established by the Norman aristocracy for their own purposes, was by the twentieth century well entrenched as the ever-present larder of the rural poor, the realm of the rough-shoot, the terrier and trap. To remove it, and furthermore to remove it at a time when the whole country was, at least in theory, on starvation rations, when the ability of Britain and indeed Europe simply to feed its own growing population was teetering on the brink, must have seemed at best deranged and at worst a mass act of deliberate homicide against the poorest and hardest working in society, comparable to the whole bloody mess that had got the continent there in the first place. Now, again, we find ourselves in a position, which should surely have been just a distant memory at this stage in the development of so-called civilization, where the ability of even the richest countries in the world to cater for the basic needs of its citizens is at issue; civilizations coalesce on the most basic level to feed themselves, and if they fail at this they perhaps do not deserve to be called civilized.

From those convenient warrens, anyway, in which the animals were kept semi-domesticated as a self-sustaining source of both food and sport – much as pheasants, partridges and grouse are today – the rabbit has spread to populate the farms and downlands of the south, the sand-duned expanses and heaths of the East Anglian coast, and all the moors and wild places of the country except for the very coldest and highest. Living on parched grass and bitter herbs, they are preyed on by raptors and larger mammals, by famine and pestilence, and always by the descendants of those responsible for their original colonies, with gun, with trap, and with biological and chemical warfare. Although the wild rabbit population has never quite recovered to its antebellum abundance, and fluctuates, declining here, increasing there, it is still populous enough to be considered a pest, both personally by anyone who attempts to grow plants for food, and legally, in that there is no closed season on shooting them. Whether the shooting seasons in fact represent the reality of the animal populations on the ground or in the air is quite another matter; the law is far too slow-moving to reflect such ever-shifting patterns, but the fact remains that rabbits are killed, in quite large numbers, at the end of a life otherwise lived without direct human intervention on land used for quite other things. The ones we do not eat will be killed anyway and simply slung over the nearest hedge.

Rabbit is almost a byproduct of vegetable farming, perhaps one of the most sustainable things we can eat and certainly one of the most sustainable meats alongside pigeon and deer; the latter, however, occupies a strange position, whereby, lacking their natural predators, the wild communities of all kinds of deer – roe, red, and fallow, the tiny muntjac and Chinese water deer alike – are regularly culled to keep populations fairly level, but the carcasses often do not find their way back into the food chain. Meanwhile, farmed venison is brought in from New Zealand and there are calls to expand its domestication in Scotland in order to meet the growing demand for game, as cooks and eaters turn away from even the best-kept farmed meat. As this might suggest, not all wild animals are equally wild. If you travel through Suffolk at the beginning of the shooting season, some months before our meal begins, you will see pheasant and partridge, dozens upon dozens, milling around seemingly without aim in fields and verges and around the corpses of their fellows, which line the road. These birds, whose tropical plumage is particularly striking amidst the tweed and dun of an East Anglian autumn and who seem to lack even the most fundamental of animal instincts, do not, of course, spring fully formed from the long grass in which they often vainly attempt to hide from creatures taller than them, but are bred almost entirely for sport. If they were bred for food, they would be subject to rather more regulation, and it might be considered cruel to despatch a partridge, say, with gun and by hand. To compound the matter, however, pheasant in particular are barely even valued as food. Released and then shot in vast numbers, stuffed carelessly into the bag still warm, many of them are already rotting by the time you come to pluck, which is considered scarcely worth the effort; of those not given away or simply tossed aside to feed the foxes, many will have their breasts cut straight from the feathered chests, the good meaty legs discarded.

At least pheasants, once released into nature, occupy a land that, if not itself wild, is not by and large kept solely for the purposes of shooting, as is the case with the grouse moors of Scotland and the north; the rearing and protection of pheasant populations is nothing compared to the all-out war waged against the delicate balance of nature which goes under the name of moorland management. Foxes and stoats, which prey on grouse chicks, are trapped and killed, as are the dwindling brown hares, which are not directly harmful to the birds but are known to sometimes carry a parasite that can be so. In sixteen-year cycles, huge areas of the surface of the moor are burnt away to manage the heathers that feed and protect grouse, so some is young and tender to eat, others tall and sheltering; other parts are drained, causing flooding in the towns and the cities lower down. All of this, strictly speaking, is permitted under the law, although the persecution and destruction of birds of prey, which continues unabated despite measures both legal and practical to prevent it, most definitely is not.

When I was vegetarian I considered myself above all this squalor; it seemed to me that, quite apart from the existential implications of feeding your animal body with the flesh of another, to participate in any way in the meat industry was to condone its worst practitioners, and that the best thing was total abstention. If everybody was vegetarian, I thought, then the horrors of crammed, disfigured chickens, of pigs packed snout to tail between metal bars, and the aerial slaughter of semi-tame idiot birds, would be over. The question of what we might do, if everybody was vegetarian, with the vast herds of pigs and sheep occupying vast portions of the British countryside, hardly occurred to me; that it would lead to the extinction of, at least, the otherwise unexploitable domestic swine now seems clear. I can't recall what exactly changed my mind, but I came gradually to believe that an active engagement is better than the disengagement of vegetarianism; in other words, that to seek out and buy meat farmed with respect for the health and wellbeing of animal, human and environment might have a wider effect than to opt out altogether. Such meat, it's true, is more expensive, but that just means that you should eat less of it, and in more interesting ways, as in our meal.

The offcuts of farmed pork are there only for ballast, with the main bulk of our ragù coming from the now genuinely wild rabbit, which can easily be got year-round from any large or rural butcher or game dealer, but which, it so happens, is perhaps at its best in the spring. While this might seem mere romantic whimsy, it is because, from summer onwards, the chemicals and hormones of sexual maturity will begin to suffuse the meat with their musk and funk. This, in uncastrated pigs, is known as boar taint: it partly causes the distinctive sheepiness of hogget and mutton and it can render older bucks quite unpalatable; so we are told, at any rate, although the brining and long cooking I normally give to rabbit mean I have never particularly noticed this. In spring, at least, unless your butcher retrieves your four rabbits from the depths of his freezer, the meat will be soft and white, though with a distinctive ripple and spring which means it could never be mistaken for chicken, even if your knowledge of animal biology is distinctly lacking and even if, as is usual in this country, their staring heads have been removed. Lay them out in front of you; we are almost ready to cook.

17

ON THE
PREPARATION
OF RABBIT

You might think we had started cooking, but it's time now to back-track a little, past the trotter stock, past that almost incidental dish of vinegared celery, past those salt-bathed potatoes and their green butter, past even the soffritto, constructed so carefully, back to the salt and to the animals, which we left, or rather will leave, to sit overnight in a nurturing brine. It's time to focus a little care and attention on to what will, after all, be the structure and the meat of this meal, as it were; it's time to look at rabbits, four of them, which you have acquired from a good butcher and which now sit, or rather lie, on your kitchen counter. These small bodies, which may well be the first entire corpses you have seen, could on a brief inspection be the bodies of any smallish mammal. I am told that the reason rabbits are always sold with the kidneys in place is that the exact position of the offal relative to the hips and shoulders is the only reliable way to tell their bodies apart from those of cats as they hang in the butcher's window; a reminder that the trust-worthy food systems and reliable chains of provenance we associate with traditional cuisines and societies are not the preserve of some bucolic golden age but are rather constantly in flux, created daily by the network of laws, customs and minute choices that govern us. To put it another way, there have always been people who have done whatever they could get away with in order to make a little money, which I suppose is news to no-one.

The kidneys, though clearly visible in the stomach cavity, are half-encased in a layer of quite solid fat (which would be called suet in a larger animal), almost the only fat you will see on the carcass, the thickness of which seems to vary widely from rabbit to rabbit and also from place to place; the rabbits we get in Suffolk, for example, seem to have much more fat than similar Norfolk animals. Whether this means that the living is easier in the south of East Anglia I do not know; I would like to get hold of some rabbits from Yorkshire, say, or from Wales, to make a proper comparison, but that can wait for another time. Alongside the kidneys and this suet you may or may not find the liver, which may or may not be especially edible. If it is yellowish or mottled then you should throw it away, but the only way to find out more is by eating it. Rabbit offal can be delicious, especially if tossed in spiced and seasoned flour then fried, crispy and pink-centred, in hot bacon fat, or made into a little salad with bitter leaves and lardo. It can also, in my experience, be absolutely foul, really unpalatably, poison-ously bitter. Here more than anywhere else you see the effects and the inconsistencies of the wild; the kidneys and the liver, as you might expect, bear the remnants of anything unpleasant that your rabbit might have eaten in its short life. Still, I'd say it was delicious perhaps eight times out of ten, so enjoy it as a treat while the rabbit is brining or cooking – just don't, perhaps, stake your meal on it.

That, in any case, is a good rule to follow when dealing with rabbit or with any wild meat at all: it is best to take it as it comes. The recipe we are following is fairly universal, but if you had planned, say, a beautiful rabbit roast in a wrap of bacon and woody herbs, or perhaps a little fricassee with asparagus and peas, then unless you had a particularly well-stocked butcher or a direct line to the warren, you would almost inevitably be disappointed; the very young rabbits required for such preparations are quite hard to come by. It is best, if you are planning ahead, to assume that you will have to stew your rabbit, which works as well with an adolescent as it does with a battle-worn old buck, tough of muscle and tendon. Once you have handled a few rabbits you will know which is which by the colour and feel of the meat as much as by the size, which can be hard to assess when you have nothing else to judge it against. Big rabbits always seem much bigger than they have any right to be, and small rabbits much skinnier. At any rate, you'll find out its particular needs when you come to cook it; for now it is enough to know that you have four rabbits and, I hope, a good sharp knife and a heavy cleaver or small hammer.

Take one of your rabbits and lay it out on a chopping board, face- or rather stomach-down, with the back legs towards you; these you will need, I'm afraid, to dislocate. Place your thumb at the base of the spine and curl your fingers round the front of the rabbit's thigh, then, bracing the one against the other, pull it sharply towards you with the hip joint as a hinge, and you should hear a crack; repeat with the other leg. Now pick up your knife, the good sharp one, and taking the left leg first, slice neatly through the dislocated joint, working from the top of the hip and down, round the surprising bodybuilder's strength of their ham, corrugated with muscle, and then out at the groin. Put the left leg to one side, flip the rabbit over, and repeat with the other leg. The shoulders are just a little harder to remove, being more neatly flush with the body, and they are also in my experience more likely to be damaged, whether by shot or dog or ferret, than are the sturdy hind legs; I had a rabbit once – a carcass, you understand – the whole front half of which had been forcibly removed by presumably quite a large animal, and which probably should not have been offered for sale as a whole rabbit. Assuming yours is in a better condition, you will need to claw your fingers behind the shoulder blade and, tugging it away slightly from the torso, insert the blade of your knife into the gap so created. Then you simply need to cut down and round, perhaps hacking a little at the oddly strong tendon that starts somewhere around the elbow, and again, flip the rabbit over and repeat.

The rabbit, you'll note, is beginning to look less like the carcass of a small mammal and more like pieces of meat, or at least the four legs you have removed and put to one side are; they could almost be packed in polystyrene and arranged on a butcher's counter. The scrawny mid-section, on the other hand, is beginning to look more and more like a dismembered corpse, especially if it has also been shot up a little. You can consider yourself lucky if there is no bleeding, bruising or laceration anywhere on your rabbit; as they are shot mainly to kill rather than specifically for the pot, there is little incentive to try and aim, say, for the head, which in any case would require a more powerful gun than those usually used on rabbits. Since the animals possess a neatly marked target in the form of the white blaze across their chests, and since they tend to rear up and display this when alarmed, you will often find that the ribcage

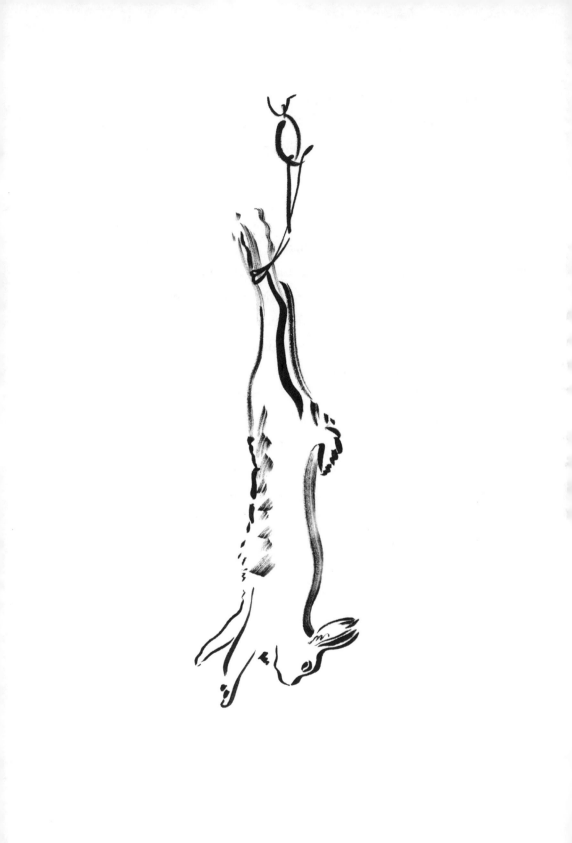

is particularly mangled, even if the limbs have escaped damage. Well, it would be a surprise if there were no signs of a violent death, no mark left by a life interrupted, and the ribcage is luckily of no real use to the cook, rabbit stock not being particularly worth making in my experience. I have had rabbit ribs in a tapas bar in Barcelona, the little racks separated out into tiny chops, floured and fried; these were lovely, and there was a slightly surreal pleasure in eating such a doll's-house cut of meat, but I am sure they must have come from the larger and more tender farmed rabbit.

If you want to see the difference that diet and lifestyle make to the eatability of a particular animal, there could be no better illustration than a farmed and a wild rabbit cooked side by side. When cookbooks inform you that rabbit tastes rather like chicken and suggests you substitute the one for the other in a given recipe, it is the farmed rabbit they are talking about, which is particularly popular in France and Spain but almost unavailable here; if you do find it, it will have been imported from one of the continental farms, where fat, inbred rabbits, all of them albino, flop lazily around and across each other, with ten or twenty to a single cage, rows and rows of cages to a barn, however many barns to a farm. Their plump, loose muscle is the product of juvenility and inactivity; darker meat, in any animal, requires both exercise and time, neither of which these near-motionless rabbits have any more of than do industrially farmed chickens. I was surprised, a couple of years ago, to be served a French farmed rabbit in the dining room of a pub in Wales otherwise known for the quality of its produce and the rigour of its approach. As no self-respecting food writer would ever recommend you use one of these unhappy beasts and no conscientious chef would ever allow one on to their menu, I don't see why farmed rabbit should be treated as acceptable; it is part, I suppose, of the general obfuscation surrounding game, whereby no-one is really sure what is wild and what is not and all we have for proof of provenance is the word of the farmer, the shooter or the game-dealer from whom we got it.

If you want a white meat that is quicker to cook then go and buy a good chicken and roast it as plainly as you dare; what we have is wild rabbit with a delicate and quite possibly badly damaged ribcage, so find the last rib on each side and cut through the flap of skin that joins it to the body, then, putting forefinger and thumb into the space you have made, pull the ribs sharply upwards, towards where the head used to be, exposing a clear section of spine. Take your heavy cleaver or more probably your hammer and your knife and cut through this. Unless you spend a lot of time splitting wood or indeed butchering meat, you will find it surprisingly difficult to wield a cleaver with much accuracy, but don't worry too much about that; a few hits in the same sort of area will do the trick. Alternatively, and much more precisely, lay the heel of your large knife in the exact place you want to cut, which will be between two vertebrae. Transferring the handle to your left hand, deliver a few smart blows to the top of the knife with your hammer and you will feel the spine easily give way. I first saw this technique, which rather neatly combines accuracy and power with a minimum of mess, being used on the pass of the Smithfield restaurant St John by the head chef, who, in between finishing plates of food and sending them out into the dining room, was portioning several large flatfish into steaks on the bone; as this requires you to split the backbone lengthways down the middle, a certain precision is needed.

Whenever I see a skilled workman set about the careful dismemberment of a corpse, whether a small fish, rabbit or bird, or a much larger ungulate, and especially when I attempt to do so myself, it always strikes me how unfair the metaphor of butchery, in the sense of a savage, unreasoned assault, is to what after all is a delicate and demanding profession. I like to think instead of the elegant dance described by Zhuangzi, in the tale of Cook Ding, who kept his knife so sharp it could glide through the space between muscles, never touching a thing. Watching the chef at St John that evening, as he unhurriedly deconstructed his pile of fish, carefully washing his hands to the wrist each time he had to go back to the pass, was like watching a surgeon at work; even the rather more brutal act of cleaving a hanging cow straight in half, it seems to me, has a certain delicacy to it. However jolly your butcher is – and they do tend to be jolly – when you look at them there is always the knowledge that they have cut with knife and cleaver and bone saw and power tool through many hundreds of bodies and can do so with consummate skill, and as such live one step closer to death than most of us do in this pampered modern world. In this fashion are my thoughts engaged while finishing this minor piece of butchery, as I use the same cleaver or combination of hammer and knife to cut off the little piece of spine that comes down from the hips to where the tail would have been, and put the trimmed saddle piece to one side with the legs. More accurately, in fact, I put it to one side with the rest of the saddle pieces, as, although I have talked you through this process one rabbit at a time, it is much more efficient to first do all of the legs, then all of the shoulders, then cut under each set of ribs, and so on; for one thing you won't have to keep picking up the cleaver or hammer, swapping hands and putting it down again, and for another, you will find, in turning yourself into a miniature production line, a certain calm rhythm that comes from doing the same thing over and over again and having the time to do it well.

Pack your rabbit pieces into a pot or a tub and cover with a cold five per cent brine, enlivened, if you like, with perhaps a little juniper, bay and cloves; we'll cook the lot together tomorrow. Sometimes, I should say, I take the saddle parts and cook them separately; if you take your sharp knife and cut the fillets from them by inserting the blade next to the spine and simply following it down and round so that neat little cigars of flesh roll off the side and on to your board, you will see that the meat is very different from that of the legs, as you might well expect. The fillets on the underside of the body, particularly, are loose and open-textured enough to squash between forefinger and thumb like the strips on the underside of a chicken breast. These saddle fillets are the only part of the rabbit that can be cooked quickly, even in fairly old animals, and it is nice, if you have a lot, to do something different with them, to fry them up for a warm salad with black pudding and chicory, or to pepper and smoke them and eat with pickles. You wouldn't, after all, stew a fillet steak together with an oxtail, and the saddle does tend, even more than the rest of the rabbit, towards dryness if not carefully cooked. Left on the bone, though, brined and then treated with caution, it braises very well, and more often than not I will stew the whole rabbit and enjoy the different textures that come from the different parts and their different uses in life.

18

ON A VERSION
OF RABBIT RAGÙ

In the morning, then, we can finally begin to cook. In a moment we will go back to that soffritto, or rather start to cook it from scratch, since we have, you'll remember, returned to that point in this rather lengthy cooking process. First, though, the rabbit needs a little work. There are those who would tell you that braising rabbit smells; all braising things smell of course, but rabbit, say its detractors, smells specifically of grassy excrement, of musk, of all the visceral animal smells we would rather keep out of our kitchen. And to be fair it does – unless you blanch it first. Drain the rabbit pieces from their brine and rinse briefly, then put them in a large pan, cover with cold water and bring quickly to a brisk boil for a minute or two. This stage will definitely smell and the rabbit will begin to expel an amount of grey scum – this is the idea. Drain, rinse again and clean out the pan, and we are, at last, ready to start with rabbit that will smell only of good things on its long journey into dinner.

Prepare your soffritto, then, and when it is at that sizzling, almost-fried stage, stir in a couple of large spoonfuls of tomato purée. We are too early for good fresh tomatoes, of course, and while tinned ones, especially whole plum tomatoes, are an indisputably fine thing, I feel that too much tomato overwhelms the rabbit. We aren't making pasta sauce; or if we are, then not that kind. No, we want the purée to sweeten, to thicken and to colour our stew but not to dominate it, and so a couple of spoonfuls are enough, stirred and fried into the vegetables until it, too, starts to sizzle and to separate, at which point you can cool the pan down again with some milk. Add about 200 millilitres of full-fat milk, which – reducing the heat – you want to gently bubble down until there is almost no liquid trace of it left, only pale fat and sweetness coating the soffritto. When you are content that this is the case, add the same amount of good white wine vinegar or perhaps double the amount of white wine; cider or its vinegar would also be suitable, but not red wine here, unless you have a particularly light one. The knee-jerk maxim of red-meat-red-wine and its opposite is not, of course, universally true. Beef and sherry, for example, are particularly happy partners, but at this time of the year I think it is appropriate to keep things light, in colour as in flavour; the trotter broth, which should at this point be warming and re-liquefying gently in another pan, will in any case add its own richness to the meal. Turn the heat up under the sauce to bring large bubbles to its surface, then reduce it slightly and let the wine or the vinegar putter away to nothing, or rather to nothing but intense flavour, melding with the tomato, the sweet-savoury milk and the vegetables. At this stage of making a stew or a ragù it is worth giving it your full attention; there will be hours, very soon, when you can let it simmer gently on the back of your stove or in a low oven, enjoying the developing smell as it slowly cooks away, but now you are laying the foundations of those smells and flavours. Keep both eyes, then, on what you are doing, and remember that you have all morning to prepare the rest of the meal.

If we were browning the meat, as for a darker, perhaps more wintery or autumnal dish, we would do so now, carefully and in small batches, putting each one aside before scraping all the bits of sticky flavour from the frying pan with the aid of more wine or vinegar, and adding meat, juices and all, to the waiting soffritto; as rabbit lacks either skin or fat to brown, I almost never do this. You would, of course, still get the caramelization of proteins and sugars, which are called Maillard reactions, but the price would be a tough outer layer of meat, which will probably not recover its tenderness even in the long braise to come; accept that rabbit is rabbit, I say, and look elsewhere, in fact to almost any other wild or domesticated meat if you want the flavours of fire and of crisp browned fat. Instead, you can just put your pieces of blanched and rinsed rabbit into the stew pan, tucking them amongst the developing sauce so that, hopefully, they nestle in it in a single layer; it doesn't matter especially if they don't but it seems neater and more pleasing that way, and it does make the panful easier to stir. Let them be coated and warmed by the contents of the pan, then add the trotter stock, enough to just cover them by perhaps a centimetre, though if the meatless bones of the ankles and wrists jut a little from the top, it won't be a problem. If there isn't enough trotter stock, just top up with some water or some wine or chicken stock; if, conversely, you have too much, just save it for another time. You now need to bring the stew to the slightest of simmers, and here you will see the virtue of the fat and the gelatine extracted from the trotters; the thickness of the dense liquid jelly is visible as it bubbles. You are told, when poaching various meats but especially the lighter, more delicate ones, to never let the liquid boil, and certainly to never let it boil hard the way we boil pasta or broccoli; to do so can irrevocably toughen the fibres of the muscle. You'll see, though, that trotter stock, if you are moderately cautious with it, is simply too thick to boil hard; the most it can manage is thick bubbles breaking lazily on its surface, and having achieved this you can prop the lid ajar on your pan and leave your stew to its own devices, returning to it only occasionally to check the level of the boil and of the liquid, to adjust and to top up and to stir as required.

There seems to be no real consensus as to how long rabbit takes to cook, which is odd. I saw a recipe some time ago in a newspaper supplement, which, recommending you cook wild rabbit with mushrooms into a sauce for ribbons of pasta, advised a cooking time of only thirty-five minutes, in which time wild rabbit would have cooked enough to be tough but nowhere near enough to be tender. Either this was a genuine mistake and should have read, say, two hours and thirty-five minutes, or the testers were ignoring the demands of both ethics and flavour and, indeed, the recipe, and using farmed rabbit meat. Whatever the case, it is a shame as the recipe states that the meat can, after this brief period of cooking, be pulled apart with two forks; if you tried to do so, being unfamiliar with cooking rabbit (as most people are), you might reasonably assume that there was something wrong with either your cooking ability or with your animal. As everyone knows that rabbit can be stringy and 'difficult to cook', you would probably, in fact, assume both and perhaps never cook rabbit again. This is a particularly extreme example, but the vast majority of recipe books, or at least the ones I have read, wildly under-estimate the time required to really braise a rabbit. An hour and a half seems the usual guideline, with the proviso that the meat should then be shreddable, or yield easily to the point of a knife, or slide off the bone with a slight tug; in my experience, which is, I think, reasonably extensive, it is more like three hours, even after the shortcuts of brining and blanching.

Three hours, then, of the slowest and most gentle of nurturing braises, during which time you can prepare the rest of this meal as well as, I don't know, have a bath, tidy up a little, decant the wine, and whatever else you do when you have people coming to share your table with you. After this – yes – the meat should yield easily to the point of a small knife inserted in the thickest part of a hind leg. In fact, try this with a few of them, given the different lives that your various rabbits will have led, and therefore the different cooking times they might require. Once you are happy with the tenderness of the flesh, you can set the pan of what should now be a quite delicious rabbit stew to one side while you decide exactly what you are going to do with it; this has more to do with personal preference, both yours and that of your imagined guests, than it does with anything else. You thought, I suppose, that we had this whole meal carefully planned, that the rabbit stew would be served with well-salted potatoes and dressed spring greens, preceded by pickled vegetables and simply grilled mackerel, and you are broadly correct; yet there are still decisions to be made, as there always are, even on the brief and final journey of your main course from the pan to the plate. Do your diners tolerate bones, for example?

*

I was once put in the awkward situation of having to prepare an entire conger eel for dinner, having never addressed such a thing before. One of my housemates at the time had brought it back from work with the idea that we would, together, transform it into a meal; he promptly went upstairs and fell asleep, and there I was with a massive lump of slimy muscle crowned at one end with a sinister maw of needling teeth. I looked, as one does, to the Internet for advice and found myself, as one does, scarcely the wiser. The first piece I read, for example, insisted that conger eel must be skinned, and furthermore that it must be skinned while still alive; the way to achieve this, apparently, is to nail the creature's head to a convenient post, presumably somewhere on your fishing boat, and to rip the thick skin off with pliers. Well, the eel I had accidentally acquired was most certainly dead and there were no pliers in the house, but there is more than one way to skin an eel, as they say. On to the next piece of advice: conger eel, I learned, are scavengers and bottom feeders and you should on no account think of eating the flesh nearest their stomachs, infested as it might be with all kinds of parasites and discoloured with the trash on which they feed. I realize now that this only meant to prohibit the actual flesh around the stomach cavity, which even in more commercially available fish can be contaminated with all kinds of wildlife, but at the time I assumed I should discard the whole of the front end of the eel. Very well, the tail end it was then. The next article I read told me that this part was so full of small, spiny bones, latticed through the dense and meaty flesh, that no-one would consider it fit for human consumption.

I was faced, then, with an apparent choice between poisoning my friends and choking them, and I must say that I chose the latter. If you are being choked, after all, at least you know that you are choking, whereas poisoning can do its devastating work silently and undetected for hours before any physical alarm is raised. In the case of particular mushrooms, for example… But I am getting away from the point, which is that not knowing what else to do, I cut the tail end of the eel into large steaks, leaving the rich and glutinous skin largely intact, and stewed these in a tomato sauce, heavy with red wine, olives and capers. The result was both meaty and briny with a remarkable intensity of flavour, but it was undeniably full of bones, the tiniest of pin-sharp bones, the kind you had, as you were eating, to constantly pick from your teeth, to chomp down on and suck the juices from, and worst, to occasionally cough from the back of your throat and disgorge quietly onto the side of the plate. I and my recently awoken housemate were fine with this, as we had to be, being jointly responsible for this fishy mess. A friend of ours joining us for dinner, who had travelled quite widely, had fished and eaten with the locals and who was used to the spiny, somewhat hands-on nature of fishermen's stews, also dug in happily. My other housemates, however, though not especially less travelled, were certainly less forgiving of this – as they saw it – barely edible mess, and chose instead to dine on tuna sandwiches, on white toast with melted cheese.

And who can really blame them? If all you intend to do at dinner or at lunchtime is to eat that particular meal and to do so with your fullest attention, then you may well be willing to grapple with such things as an entire crab, boiled and served with a bowl of mayonnaise, a great pile of spiced and fried chicken wings, or

183

indeed a pot full of jointed rabbit, slow-cooked in trotter stock and sharp, savoury juices. If, on the other hand, you have better things to do than pick scraps of meat from the back of your teeth, and more things to talk of than lunch itself, then you might wish for a little more convenience in your meals. This being the case, you could, once your rabbit stew has cooked just enough to be painless to the touch, begin to shred the flesh from the different joints, discarding the hollow and well-boiled bones and returning the scraps of meat to the waiting pan of sauce. If you did so, the rich ragù you had left would be best served, in our case, spooned across and between the potatoes, more of a dressing than a centrepiece as such; it might be even better tossed through fat ribbons of freshly made pasta, topped with a sharp grated cheese and eaten alongside a bitter and peppery salad. Each meal you make carries within it the ghosts of other meals, and you could drive yourself to distraction trying to cater for them all; best, I think, to stick to our original plan and, your diners willing, serve chunks of rabbit still clinging to the fragile bones; together you can suck them clean.

19

ON EATING

I often think that there is no real verbal compliment that can honestly be paid to food, at least at the time of eating; anything more than a greasy thumbs-up and a quick smile in between chews betrays itself as empty words, and really the rhythmic clink of cutlery on crockery under a sort of silent hum of concentration is the best response of all. Whatever compliment is paid though, however much your eaters enthuse and ask you for the recipe, the time spent eating and the joy elicited never seem quite commen surate to the time invested in cooking. All those hours of chopping and slicing and pounding, of braising, boiling and whipping – and that's just the hands-on part. Think of the time spent fermenting, brining, drying, ageing, the time catching and landing the mackerel, digging and planting and sowing; think of the life the rabbit lived, months or even years before anyone thought of shooting or trapping it. Then, of course, there are the recipes, the stories that we started thinking about a long time before this meal began, which are both the most basic form of writing about food and the most refined and complex, each one capable of carrying hundreds or even thousands of years of history within a few sparse lines.

In this country especially, where almost nothing, plant or animal, is truly native, where our connections to our own traditions seem, at some point, to have been irrevocably severed, and where, through a combination of subjugation and conquest, trade and war, spices, fruits and cured delicacies have so often found their way from every end of the earth, every recipe is always pointing to something else. It might express the family background of the author, their travels or interests; it might, on the other hand, express the vastness of a now-lost empire or the particular climate of a few miles of the Mediterranean coast. It could, most likely, contain all of these things and more. If, for example, you begin a recipe with two large onions, sliced, then you are asking for something which would be impossible had the Roman Empire not spread itself across and around the sea, and to what were then the edges of the world; add a pinch of chilli flakes and some tinned tomatoes to the mix, and the edges of that world expand, heading westwards and back aboard the Santa Maria. A few threads of saffron expands them in the opposite direction, in the footsteps of the ancient Persians, whose civilization reached from India right to the edge of Europe, while a piece of gurnard, say, or perhaps monkfish or squid, sends them plunging to the dark depths of the sea. You could be cooking anywhere in the world, even in a small kitchen in East Anglia, and you would be not just reaching out to those distant places and times but touching them with your hands. Accidentally, too – since I picked those few ingredients at random – you are reaching out to Marseilles and to the fine fish soup of the south of France.

Recipes of recent provenance might have a distinct author or at least a chain of authors, of inspiration and ingredients handed from kitchen to kitchen, and these authors will of course have stories of their own, of how it happened that they stumbled upon this partic- ular preparation of raw materials, of where they did so and why, and so on. Whether all or indeed any of this is – or even should be – apparent in the eating is quite another matter. When I read a recipe which the author stresses is their own unique and distinctive take on perhaps a traditional family recipe or, worse, on a recipe that they have encountered while on holiday somewhere, I swiftly lose my appetite, even if all they have done is added or substituted in a slightly more fashionable spice, a foraged herb, or an obscure and unpronounceable cheese. I am no culinary purist, and certainly do not believe that there is only one perfect and unchangeable itera- tion of every dish you could imagine, but the mania for ownership of recipes, the insistence on solitary creative genius as the driving force in cuisine, is one I really cannot understand. Recipes, like all stories, are the work of many hands over many generations, and to participate in this process in whatever way should be its own reward. In many cases, in fact, the sign that you have done so well is that nobody notices your input; that, far from clamouring for recog- nition, your cooking melds seamlessly into the dish's long history, which at times, it seems, you can feel the weight of as you eat.

I am not sure what it is about some flavours that makes them seem to resonate in this way. Lawrence Durrell writes of the taste of black olive, as 'old as cold water', which, while not strictly true, olives requiring a great deal of human intervention in order to become edible, is certainly evocative. I mentioned before how celery seed tastes somehow ancient to me, stemming from a time when herbs and spices were as much medicine and magic as food. Certainly some cuisines bear the marks within themselves of great clashes of cultures and of particular moments in history. Go to Spain, for example, and you will see everywhere memories of the Inquisition in solid form, in the mountain hams, chorizos and sausages which hang in their hundreds in every tapas bar, bodega and restaurant; in times when anti-Semitic and anti-Islamic feelings were at their height, the Catholic Inquisition could and did demand to search your larder, to check that it contained the pork products forbidden to the other Abrahamic religions.

To pick another example, the cuisine of Sicily, which can be distinguished from the (by no means homogenous) cooking of mainland Italy by the enthusiastic use of spices and fruit with meat and fish, and by the rococo exuberance of its pastry and desserts, as much as it can be linked to it by the flash of brazen simplicity and the absolute ubiquity of the anchovy, wears its history very much on its sleeve. The earliest surviving European cookbook, Archestratus' *Art Of Luxury*, comes from Sicily, at the time a Greek colony and before that the richly abundant home of the one-eyed Cyclopes. Since then the island has been invaded, subjugated or simply bartered by or between Romans, Vandals, Byzantines, Normans and Arabs, and by German, Spanish and French royalty, and you could, if you ate your way around the island, find traces of all of these. Most obviously, perhaps, you might eat Trapani couscous, an Italianized but still direct descendant of the North African dish, which may in fact have been the origin of pasta; more generally you might note the supple and almost chewy ice-cream made in the Arabian style, the use of anchovy in place of salt as the Romans used garum, the Spanish love of chilli and heat. If you look in fact at

Archestratus' book, or at least at the surviving fragments of it, you might think, with the emphasis given to freshness, simplicity and quality of ingredients, to going to the market to select the best you could find, and to the rejection of the heavy, complicated sauces and cookery then popular amongst the rich, that you were reading a manifesto for modern Sicilian cuisine rather than one from its very beginning.

If – to return to the point – you were to eat, say, a bowl of pasta *con le sarde* with its pine nuts, saffron and raisins dotted between the Mediterranean sardines and wild fennel found everywhere in Sicily, without knowing anything about what you were eating, its history or that of the island from which it comes, would you in fact lose anything by this ignorance – would you enjoy your meal any less? Probably not. A lunch or a dinner, especially one enjoyed at the start of the vegetable year – when all kinds of new flavours, plants and ideas begin to spring up and finally break the monotony of the long dark of winter – is not an academic exercise or even a piece of gallery-bound art, all the better when extensively annotated, to be chewed over. It is, rather, there to be eaten, which is to say, destroyed – and will be destroyed however much and at whichever intellectual level it is appreciated first. Such is the lot of the cook. You might have served up in your eyes a masterpiece, a dish which expressed, shall we say, everything you thought there was to say about potato salad, but still, down it goes, destroyed just as quickly as might have been a bowl of any potato salad in the world, if not more so. 'But it's clever!' you want to cry. 'It's a fish course with no fish... it's an entirely homemade facsimile of a Snickers... it is the absolute perfection of sausage...' And nobody cares; they are too busy eating. At least, I suppose, you always know that your work is ephemeral, that it walks hand-in-hand with time on its way towards death. If nothing you make is designed to last more than ten or fifteen minutes, there is no point in aiming for perfection and you are therefore free to concentrate on more trivial things like interest and enjoyability, and whether what you do brings pleasure to those you encounter as you go about your life. Or so I always think when finally, having spent some hours in the kitchen, served up drinks and pickles and starters and at last a pot of rabbit stew to a roomful of friends who are perhaps a little drunk by now, I sit down and watch the work of days demolished in a few short minutes.

If I am eating someone else's food, in a restaurant, with other professional cooks or at least enthusiastic eaters (most of my friends being either one or the other), then all I really want to talk about is the food – perhaps moving on to the wine once we have said all there is to say about the food. We will – having probably photo-graphed it first – pick it up and prod at it, tearing off bits of kale, say, with our hands, chewing and sucking it to try and extract the maximum flavour and to work out thereby how it might have been cooked and dressed, how it might be recreated, how it might be improved. I am aware, of course, that this is not especially sociable behaviour, as becomes clear when there is someone present who wants to have something more closely resembling a normal conver-sation, and perhaps also wishes not to have bits of their lunch stolen unannounced from their plate; but then when you cook for a living eating is never entirely sociable – it is research. I quite enjoy eating alone, especially at lunchtime, which you might think would be best for research, but it does mean you get to try fewer things. Besides, unless you are going to sit taking notes and photographs throughout your whole meal, a suitable dining partner and the discussion that ensues is the best way to keep your lunch in your mind. It is possible, by yourself, to eat almost an entire meal without really noticing what you are doing; another person helps you stay focused, though you should perhaps give other reasons when inviting someone to lunch.

As I was saying, while I like restaurants and I like eating in them, I don't do so to enjoy myself as such, however much I might in fact enjoy myself. I actually find some aspects of the whole restaurant experience quite stressful, especially the often-interminable wait for the bill. No, if I want to do what a lot of people seem to go to restaurants in order to do – to use the food and the table simply as a focal point around which to gather a few friends and to lull them into contentment, the better to spend a few lazy hours – then I would rather cook at home; I know that the food will be good and that it will get out of the way. We'll enjoy it, of course, and probably talk about it a little, or more likely a lot, but that'll be it and we'll move on to other things. It should not be the kind of food that demands attention, that comes wrapped in a thousand anecdotes and sits heavy in the stomach with the weight of history; it should be food that is so simple and so old that we forget it might even have had a beginning. There is a whole subgenre of folklore consisting of what we might call origin myths for various dishes and cooking methods, ranging from the simple and implausible – the man who set his pigsty on fire and discovered crackling springs to mind – to the fully fleshed story, my favourite being the one behind the curiously named Stone Soup.

Once upon a time, the story goes, a poor man, perhaps a mendicant or just a beggar, was travelling through the mountains and came across a small town set with its back hunched against the cliffs. He might well have expected little in the way of charity in such a place, but he made his way boldly to the main square and there set out his stall. 'I have here,' he said to the few loiterers around the fountain, removing a small rock from his bag, 'I have here a magic stone; just boil it up with water, plain water from the well, and it turns it into soup – excellent soup! I lack only a fire, and a pan.' The few loiterers had by this time turned into a slightly larger crowd, novelty being hard to come by in this particular mountain town, and one of them, sensing that this would be worth his time, went immediately to the taverna for a pan, while another started building a fire.

Once the pot was filled, the traveller threw in his stone and they settled down to wait. A few bottles of wine had been brought back from the taverna with the pan, and so any initial suspicion of the stranger was forgotten as he told them tales of distant lands beyond the mountains and of the various monsters and wonders he had seen there. After the soup had been simmering for around twenty minutes, the traveller (having borrowed a ladle along with the pan) gave it a taste and pronounced it good. 'But of course it would be even better with perhaps a few beans – just to make it go a little further, you understand. What is a handful of beans between brand-new friends?' A few were quickly found and thrown into the pot, which again was left to simmer, and more wine was fetched. Again, after a couple more bottles, the traveller gave the soup a try and pronounced it good – better than good! 'Imagine how good it would be with just a little salumi, a little spice and fat against the mountain cold.' The night was, it must be said, beginning to come down, and some of the loiterers beginning to shiver. Someone brought out a little brandy — against the mountain cold — and more stories and jokes, which seemed to be getting a little more rambling and obscene, were passed around alongside it, and the widow, who made in her cellar the finest salumi in the mountains, brought out a few links of sausage.

Well, the next time the soup was tried — by the innkeeper, the traveller now willing to share the task — it was declared excellent, but just in need of some greens, a good handful of greens, and perhaps (the innkeeper considering himself something of a gourmet, or perhaps a gourmand, never having been sure of the difference) a little vinegar, some parsley, a sprinkle of red pepper — perfect! Such a miracle, this magic stone! Everyone agreed, and the traveller, fishing out the stone, carefully washing and drying it and returning it to his bag, shared out his soup among the whole town, who thanked him sincerely and, since they considered themselves both shrewd and perhaps a little suspicious, but not, when it comes down to it, inhospitable, offered the traveller a bed for the night once the drinking had finished. The innkeeper, growing voluble, even offered the traveller the hand of his daughter, which was, with regret, politely declined.

If you had been walking into the town the next day, you might have noticed a poor man, perhaps a mendicant or a beggar, leaving through the main gates like a departing hero, and seen him, once he thought he was alone, take a small rock from his bag and toss it unconcernedly to one side as he continued on his way.

20

ON FOLLOWING
RECIPES

Now, stone soup is still known by this name in its Portuguese iteration, but the story exists in various forms in several different traditions, with the ingredients changing as appropriate to place and time. Even the stone is not constant, swapped in some versions for an axe-head, a piece of wood or perhaps a handful of nails; you might imagine in fact that stone soup is simply another name for soup – which it is of course. Certainly no-one expects you, in constructing stone soup, to follow the exact letter of the recipe such as it is; rather, with no method to speak of, no particular technique beyond the most basic of simmers, it is one to be followed in spirit, adjusting base ingredients, spices, aromats and seasoning, consistency and serving temperature to suit the mood of the weather and your guests. As the only real requirement is a pot proverbially available to all but the very poorest in society, this particular recipe is an easy one to improvise around, to get to grips with the demands of your ingredients and your appetite rather than the words on the cookbook page – but really this is the case with all recipes.

What, after all, is a recipe, when it comes down to it? A list of ingredients or a particular method? A set of instructions to be followed by the author as much as the reader, or a collection of notes from the field, observations jotted down after the fact? However many cookery books you read, you will find few recipes that really teach you new techniques, that really justify the space devoted to their method. On the contrary, you will find the same steps, the same words – the same recipes, essentially – repeated again and again, even within the same book, with only the most minor of variations. An extra vegetable here, some more spice there, meat of various kinds browned or unbrowned, different colours of wine or vinegar or stock, and so on and so forth; all of these original recipes – which, in the case of a bad cookery book, have not even been tested properly – conspiring to sustain the idea that recipes, rather than representing one brief moment in the course of a long conversation between cook and ingredients, are carved by experts in immutable stone.

Someone asked me once how we made our scrambled eggs. As I started to explain that while you could do so very slowly, in a lazy stirring motion over an extremely low heat, we, being a busy and short-handed café, took the opposite approach, cooking them in a hot pan with a frantic whip of the wrist (I am perhaps verbalizing what at the time I only gestured), they interrupted: no, they meant, did we add cream or milk? Of course we didn't, and still don't, but they had missed the point. Once you have learned to scramble eggs or to cook a risotto or to stew rabbit, you can add milk or spices or cheese or whatever else you feel like; of course, by that point you might not want to, having learned to appreciate the simplicity of the ingredients themselves. For example, that rabbit stew recipe – the one, in fact, that we are now tucking into – is one that I almost never cook any more; I don't think I have done in over a year. It's not that I no longer cook rabbit (if anything I cook it more), as much that my now-standard recipe is a lot simpler, or at least requires a little less planning. When I started making that stew, though, I was enamoured of the cooking of Marcella Hazan, from whose recipe for ragù bolognaise the base of our own recipe has wandered only slightly, and I was obsessed furthermore with cooking rabbit of the most perfect juiciness, with defeating in a way the pains and the rigours of the rabbit's own life, with rendering it absolutely tender in its afterlife. While the ingredients, then, were fairly easily settled upon, it was the technique — the brining, the blanching, and the final long braise in that good rich stock — that occupied most of my time. I used ham stock for a while, which really just made everything taste of ham, before realizing that the almost flavourless jelly exuded by boiled pigs' feet was the answer.

Having cooked the dish a number of times, and having achieved something close to perfect juiciness at least once or twice — with something like rabbit you can never really hope for more consistency than that — I eventually got bored of it. Now, in case you were wondering, I just cook my rabbits in soured cream without even a soffritto, just a few cloves of sliced garlic cooked in butter, maybe a handful of sauerkraut and perhaps some chicken stock to fill in the rest of the flavour. I do still brine them first, but more out of habit than anything else. Using slightly-past-its-best double cream inoculated with a little live yoghurt — which as well as thickening the dairy provides a welcome burst of acid to cut through its rich fats — this is, for me at least, quite an economical dish and has the added advantage of not filling the kitchen with the heavy steam of boiling bones for what seems like days on end, but must in fact be only hours. You might feel perhaps that I have tricked or at least misled you into spending so much time on this and other tasks, in which case I can only apologize. The rabbit stew we originally created was a much better example of a stew, or a ragù or a daube, and having learned to cook the more complex dish you can now more fully appreciate the simple one – which, as it happens, goes equally well with salsa verde, although you may like to introduce a little more dill into the mixture to keep the stew company as its flavours move further east.

No, we were better off with our original stew, I think, and not just because this soured-cream construction – which I currently prefer and which you could, therefore, argue is better – is taken directly with almost no changes from a recent cookbook. What, after all, is a stew? (I never normally ask so many rhetorical questions, but this point in the meal, when we drink a little more and digest our stew, seems to be the time for them.) All it is in terms of ingredients is protein-flavoured liquid. I suppose you could omit the flavourings, by which I mean all the vegetables of the soffritto or mirepoix as well as any spices or herbs, and still have something recognizably a stew; as even the infamous black broth of the Spartans contained a little vinegar to cut through the blood-thickened pork stock, that would seem a little puritanical, however. I'm not sure, in any case, if something with less than three ingredients can really be called a recipe.Those three it is then, meat, vegetable and stock – but without any method they don't constitute a recipe either. The clue, you might think, is in the name: the method of making a stew is that you stew things, but of course there is a little more to it than that. An Irish Stew is really simple to make, requiring nothing of the cook except the layering of ingredients in a pot and then a long slow boil, but most other stews are defined by what you do to each component: browning the protein or not, sweating or caramelizing or roasting the vegetables, using stock or water or reduced wine or vinegar or beer or some combination of these as your liquid medium. A daube, for example, properly speaking, is a stew with the meat left unbrowned, while a beef bourguignon, as the name suggests, must be drowned in Burgundy wine.

What you need, once you have learned how to cook a stew, is not recipe upon lengthy recipe for variations from across the globe and the ages, but instead terse suggestions – along the lines of sherry and unbrowned beef, celery and seared lamb, salt cod and orange – which can be neatly fitted into what you already know about stew and, more importantly, what you have to hand and how much time you have to cook it in. After all, no-one knows this as well as you do, and it is beyond the scope of the average cookbook to second-guess.

Why then, you might ask, do I have so many cookery books, and why, too, do I keep buying more? One answer, which would not be inaccurate, is that I like looking at the pictures; in fact I think I cook more from photographs than I do from written recipes, but that's not the whole of it. Say, rather, that I like to read the stories, even if I always know the ending – which is, broadly speaking, 'and they all had lunch'. Like a fairytale, though, or a favourite book read dozens of times, the fact that you know what lies ahead does not lessen the pleasure of getting there; to put it another way, everyone obsesses about spoilers and plot, which always follow a more-or-less formulaic scheme, thereby missing the pleasure of the words they are reading. I remember finding it odd, studying Shakespeare at school, that the brief lives of Romeo and Juliet are laid out in detail by the Chorus before the first scene has begun, and that this story, which manages at the same time to seem the product of inexorable fate and the most ridiculous string of coincidence and misfortune, was never new to even its first audiences, even had they not been familiar with the writer's sources or with the remarkably similar story of Pyramus and Thisbe which he elsewhere dramatizes. The plot — the original, unique plot — was for Shakespeare never the point; it was, rather, the particular iteration with all its oddities and joys, which gripped.

Leaving Shakespeare aside for a moment, perhaps a better model for practical cookery writing would be one of those picture books with the pages divided horizontally into three, each repre-senting, from top to bottom, the head, the torso and the legs of various anthropomorphized animals, arranged in line so that you can make, one moment, a goat with the body of a crocodile and the legs of a pig, the next, the majority of a horse crowned with a cockerel's head. Flip the pages idly along, each with a different protein, vegetable or liquid represented, and there you have your ingredients, missing only everything that makes a recipe a recipe. But just because no particular recipe can be considered the final word on its subject does not mean that the results of each experi-ment in these intermittent stages are not worth setting down; just because they repeat themselves in the familiar mantras of a nursery rhyme or folk tale does not mean they are wasting time. Instead they are marking it, since everything to do with food and with eating, it sometimes seems to me – that bizarre practice whereby to keep ourselves alive we force the decaying remains of animals and of plants into our salivating mouths – is a ritual bound intricately to the hesitant dance of life and death. The comforting tick of knife against board and, behind it, the murmur – chop your onion, then add it to the pan with a splash of oil, dice the carrots and the celery and add these too... – can act with the stove barely even on as a spell to keep out the cold, and to occupy fully the long hours before the final dark.

21

ON COOKING
WITH BLOOD
AND COOKING
WITH EGGS

Having cooked with salt, with water, with flesh and with bones, it seems only right to spend a little time with blood, which so far we have barely mentioned, the infamous black broth of the ancient Spartans excepted. This soup, concocted, as far as can be gathered, from the stock of a pig's leg mixed with simmering blood and a little vinegar, was notorious throughout the ancient world, with one gourmand remarking on tasting it that he now knew why the Spartans did not fear death. Although I have yet to make it, this assessment does strike me as perhaps unfair; for one thing, blood, at least in sausages, black pudding, boudin noir, morcilla and the like, is delicious, and for another, their soup probably didn't contain very much. It seems clear that the blood was being used not as a main flavouring or even, particularly, as a protein source, but rather as a thickening agent. If so, the soup, far from being some monstrous, primitive hellbroth, was in fact a distant ancestor of the delicate modern Greek and Turkish *avgolemono*, egg-and-lemon, which appears also under various names in the cuisines of Italy and the Balkans, and can be a sauce or dip but is more often a kind of broth containing chicken.

To make it, you prepare your soup as usual, with stock, vegetables, bits of broken pasta, rice, beans, and whatever else you happen to have, this being very much a method or perhaps a genre of soup rather than a recipe as such, and meanwhile beat an egg together with some lemon juice in a little bowl. When the time comes to eat, you add a ladleful of hot soup to this bowl, whisking the contents vigorously, and then, still whisking, pour the lot back into the pot. As you keep it over a gentle heat, stirring enough to ensure that it does not boil, you will notice the soup gloss and thicken to a velvet sheen; this is the egg, which would simply have scrambled if added unmixed to the hot broth, doing its work.

When introduced to heat or to air, egg likes to thicken, and so, as the Spartans knew, does blood. In many ways, in fact, blood likes to behave in exactly the same way as egg. I am reliably told, though I have never done so, that you can make meringues out of blood and sugar, whipping the two into a pinkly clouded mass; I have made a fairly successful hollandaise sauce using blood instead of yolks and, placing it on top of poached eggs, ham and toasted breakfast muffins, called it Eggs Dracule. Blood, then, is if anything more versatile than the eternally useful egg, as it can stand in for either the white or the yolk as the occasion demands.

Eggs themselves are little miracles – so much more useful than chickens. Neatly packaged and compartmentalized by nature, they are, appropriately, a starting point in the wider world of food, fed to babies and invalids and anyone who needs to (re)learn the pleasures of eating; if not actually easy to cook, they are the first ingredient many of us work with, a fact we pay homage to every day at breakfast. 'Go to work on an egg,' they said, and it was good advice – but they're even better for long, lazy mornings. The meal of brunch could not exist without the emulsifying presence of the egg to combine its disparate parts, its salads and sandwiches, hashes, leftovers and toast. Egg (or more particularly its yolk) is a great matchmaker.

What magician first made a mayonnaise? What was she (probably not he) doing? How did she know? It can't have taken a Blumenthal to work out the effect that breadcrumbs or ground nuts (which we still occasionally use in bread sauce, in salsa romesco, in the various alchemies of Georgian cuisine) would have when thrown into a stew, but to bring together two liquids and end up with something thicker than either? We can only bow down to this long-lost innovator, who should be the patron saint of the kitchen. But perhaps you don't make mayonnaise at home (you should); think about a cooked yolk then – the way, mixed with cream, it bakes or simmers into a silken whole, occupying a perfect liminal space between solid and liquid. A well-made quiche, quivering plainly in a buttery shell, is a beautiful thing, a bad one a disaster. Eggs are difficult to cook. When such things were still fashionable, a soufflé used to be considered a real test of skill – Anthony Bourdain describes the soufflé station as the ultimate ordeal of his education at the confusingly named CIA (Culinary Institute of America) – which is a testament to the tricky versatility of the egg. Essentially a yolk-enriched béchamel mixed with extraordinary amounts of air, a soufflé showcases the egg white, its ability to become something both extremely rich and toyingly light, decadently ephemeral. This might seem to circle around French cooking, but that is no coincidence; if there's one area of cuisine that the French can really claim to have raised to an art, it's egg cookery. From the humble omelette to the most delicate creations of the *saucier*, the egg, more than butter, wine or garlic, is the real hero of the French kitchen, the symbol of its gift for complete transformation.

Although the thickening and liaising effects of blood have clearly been known since antiquity, as showcased not just in the thoroughly cooked sausages and puddings found wherever in the world there is blood and heat, but also in dishes such as jugged hare, the Vietnamese duck blood soup, and of course that infamous black broth where it is much more recognizably a bodily fluid, it is only quite recently – in the last decade, in fact – that more precise research has been done into its egg-like properties in the kitchen. I always find it strange when I realize how little is known to science about such a basic aspect of human and indeed animal life as eating; it seems especially so in this case though, because the comparison is so natural. Of course blood cooks like egg; they are almost the same thing, each of them an echo of the primordial soup and each playing an appropriately rich part in folklore and in fairytale. As the excellent paper from the Nordic Food Lab, which was the first to my knowledge to fully explore this link and which certainly led me to do so, puts it, blood of any kind is elemental, both mystical and mundane; it is a description that could apply equally well to the egg, which is, as M.F.K. Fisher reminds us, 'one of the most private things in the world before it is broken'. It is certainly true that a whole egg is one of the hardest ingredients to assess, either raw or cooked. A friend of mine, when working the evening shift at a hotel, used to keep himself amused by hard-boiling eggs and placing them at random amongst the raw ones left ready for break-fast service the next day; although you could probably, if you were

paying attention, notice the difference in your hand between a raw
and a boiled egg, it would certainly be easy not to when scrambling
or frying or constructing omelettes from hundreds at a clip.

Although the eggs you buy in shops are scanned for oddities and
defects, double-yolked eggs are not uncommon, and I remember
being sent as a matter of emergency to the cornershop when my
mother, breaking the habit of a lifetime, cracked – too late – a
rotten egg, not into an intermediary cup but directly into the
mixture of what would have been a birthday cake; I don't know
if that was down to her own oversight or that of the shop, but
although I haven't encountered a rotten egg since, I can still smell it
now. Perhaps the most unpleasant variation on this theme is when
you get an egg that has been fertilized or in some more mystical
way begun to develop towards its intended natural goal, the result
being not a virgin birth but an eggshell which is, appropriately
enough I suppose, full of blood. I have not attempted to cook with
this, though if I did I would want to do so thoroughly, more from
squeamishness than anything else.

In general, of course, eggs barely need cooking at all. A raw
egg, in fact, or at least a yolk, is a perhaps unexpectedly decadent
ingredient, both for its enriching work behind the scenes and when
it occasionally takes centre stage; chopped raw beef appropriately
seasoned with pickles and condiments, crowned with a raw egg
yolk and served with chips, is really one of the finest meals it is
possible to eat, especially if they let you mix it all together yourself.
Usually I'm rather sceptical of these do-it-yourself meals, which
seem gimmicks designed to remove responsibility from the professional kitchen and place it with amateur diners. The seasoning of

a steak tartare, however, is such a personal thing that I am happy to make an exception – particularly as I like mine with levels of ketchup and capers that most people would consider unreasonable, but which, in any case, are toned down by the emollient effect of that raw egg yolk.

I have never actually handled fresh animal blood, which since the days of so-called mad cow disease has been quite difficult for the average consumer and even for the professional kitchen to get hold of; I find it unlikely, should I manage to do so, that it would effectively tame and bind the disparate elements of a steak tartare quite so successfully as an egg. I am certain, on the other hand, that reconstituted dried blood – which, unless you have a direct line to the slaughterhouse, you will have to be content with – would not. However carefully you rehydrate it, slowly whisking the exact amount of blood-temperature water into the rusty black powder, it always seems to retain a sort of dustiness, an ancient sense of not-quite-edibility, strongly redolent of scabs and clots and of the grave and, less fancifully, of iron; although this is of course part of the particular charm of blood, it is perhaps a little much when completely uncooked and unadorned. Best, I think, to cook it as smoothly as possible, that is to say in a custard, that mixture of yolk and of dairy that is one of the finest examples of egg cookery, and which is also, when appropriately flavoured, ideally suited to dessert, a course I'm sure you thought I had, until now, completely forgotten about.

Like a lot of professional cooks, I am fairly ambivalent about eating desserts and not especially skilled at making them; in a large kitchen, pastry and its associated arts occupy a realm entirely other to that of the rest of the menu – either physically, temporally or simply by temperament – requiring as they do a degree of calm, precision and repetition which is alien to many cooks. In a small kitchen, on the other hand, a lot of sweet things – ice-cream, viennoisserie and the like – will simply be bought in. It is something, in other words, that you have to go out of your way to learn, and I never really did. In most cases I would rather have cheese, but I know that not everyone feels the same way and it is nice to have a few simple things up your sleeve, preferably of the kind that don't take days of stirring and straining and chilling to achieve – though if you can stomach these things and possess or can access an ice-cream machine, then learning to make your own is really very satisfying and impresses everyone, as well as being another excellent example of the culinary work of eggs.

Something like a mousse or a posset would do the job, I think, and I am not convinced that anyone wants anything more at the end of a meal than a small pot of either a final richness or cleansing citrus, but it is blood that we are talking about. We could use blood instead of the eggs in a mousse, of course, although my earlier comments stand on the subject of raw dried blood; we could also perhaps make a blood orange posset, but having come this far, that would feel a little like cheating. Let's instead take refuge in something you can at least tell your diners is a traditional dessert made with the blood of pigs, and make a southern Italian *sanguinaccio dolce*, a sort of sweet black pudding which would once have been the treat of the pig-killing season and can take various forms, from a warm custard to a firm sausage which closely resembles its savoury cousin. This version, though, turns it into a sort of sct pudding, fudgy, spoonable and almost black, as well as, in a sop to more modern palates, adding a lot more chocolate than is usual. What we end up with is rather more of a chocolate pudding thickened with blood than it is a genuine blood pudding, but it is probably none the worse for that.

It is always best to be suspicious when cooks start telling you that something is very quick or very easy to make, or at least to bear in mind that their idea of quick and easy might be different to yours. That being said, this really is both very easy and quite quick to make, assuming you have access to dried blood and to a reliable thermometer, as of course everyone has in the age of the Internet. All you have to do is to take thirty-five grams of your dried blood and place it in a heatproof bowl with 100 grams of lukewarm water — a millilitre of water, as I'm sure you're aware, weighs a gram, and scales are usually much more accurate than measuring jugs — and whisk them thoroughly together until quite smooth, which might take a while. It's just about long enough, in fact, to reflect that in the not-too-distant past all such whisking would have been done not with neat balloons of wire but with more or less haphazard bundles of twigs, and that simply beating a bowl of cream to soft peaks might have taken upwards of an hour, if not to finally conclude that the steady march of progress, amongst all its other efficiencies, to an extent eliminates daydreaming. In any case, you can test the smoothness of your blood by rubbing a drop between thumb and forefinger. It won't, as I said, be entirely smooth, but it should not contain tangible grains. This being so, you can add everything else to the bowl of blood, which is to say 100 grams each of light muscovado sugar, a reasonably low grade of olive oil and double cream, and twice as much chopped good dark chocolate. Originally the chocolate element would have more likely come from cocoa powder, which I might try if I ever get hold of some fresh blood; as it is, I think one bitter black dust is enough. Stir all of these things together and set the bowl over a pan gently simmering of water, big enough to contain it comfortably, small enough that the base of the bowl is clear of the liquid; keep on stirring, in a gentle sort of figure-of-eight, while the sugar dissolves and the chocolate melts and the blood thickens, until the whole melds into a sort of perfect unction, or to be more precise until it reaches sixty-seven degrees centigrade. When it does, pour the lot into a waiting jug and then into six little pots; put these into the fridge to await the end of the meal.

22

ON CHEESE
AND COFFEE

Most cookery books don't, I think, talk enough about meals, which seems strange. I suppose, with the decline first of breakfast and then of lunch, the meal is no longer the basic unit of eating, the procession of course after course being overtaken in importance by the dish. Look into any book of recipes from the Forties, the Fifties, or even later, and you are likely to see, alongside the admittedly simpler recipes, lists of menus using them in a variety of contexts, for different occasions and through different times of the year. Even as late as 1986 – the year I was born, as it happens – Elisabeth Luard felt it necessary, compiling *European Peasant Cookery*, to include at the end of almost every recipe suggestions for how to precede and follow it, and with what salad and what wine to accompany it; this seems to the modern reader both quaint and rather touching, as well as actually quite useful. You might argue, I suppose, that in times of hardship – whether under the active fog of war, or simply the general privation that has, throughout human history, characterized the lives of those whose cuisines we now borrow – to cook for one's own pleasure might seem pathological, if not actively wasteful, but to cook for other people is always both sane and kind; in some cases it might be revolutionary. A quick glance over the history of the Jewish peoples, for example, as expressed in their culinary traditions, shows each of their ritual meals to be freighted with the memory of both tremendous sorrow and of fortitude; how much more so when they were forced, as has happened again and again, to conduct these meals in secret for fear of persecution and of death.

To cook for other people, or at least to share your table with them, is always a political or symbolic act, and it is no coincidence that so many cultures and peoples throughout history have had the principles of guest-right and of hospitality enshrined as the most fundamental of codes – the sort of natural, unalienable laws by which even the gods must abide. In more vicious times, before the semblance of civilization had settled over the greater part of the world and when any stranger could turn out to be an enemy, there had to be some safe space where you might relax in the knowledge that, at least for the moment, no-one was trying to rob or to kill you; that space, appropriately enough, was the dining table. Time and again we see the injunction that once you have shared at least your bread and wine with someone you are obligated to them and they to you. Glance through a collection of Norse myths, for example, and you will see story after story in which the chief of the gods himself wandered the barren winter landscape in disguise, the better to check and to punish infringements of this rule. Still today we forge friendships, relationships and partnerships over the dining table; even the most backbiting of offices or the most bickering of families can call a truce for long enough to eat Christmas dinner in peace, if not to make it all the way to coffee. I like to think that the haste with which good restaurants bring you bread at the start of your meal is to stave off any fights which might otherwise break out over the empty table. In fact, there are few things more unpleasant in the day-to-day life of a restaurant than a hungrily angry customer – especially one who has waited a while for their dining partners – for whom the menu is wrong, the seats are wrong, the wines are wrong, and especially the waiter is wrong about almost everything, including such basic details as whether the kitchen is in fact open for business.

The reward (though I say this having rarely had to deal personally with customers) is seeing the absolute change wrought by even just a little food, by a starter of soup or salad or pickles or perhaps a piece of simply grilled mackerel, which might be compared to the clearing of dense fog or to the sun emerging from distant clouds. It is easy to mock people who let their appetites rule their moods to such an extent, but then, why shouldn't they? When you eat, after all, you are not just doing so for pleasure but are quite literally taking in life, that of the strong-swimming mackerel, the fast-running rabbit, the pale celery growing damply in earth. When you feed people you are literally granting them perhaps a few more hours of life, taken up though that may be by eating; that at least is what I tell myself when on occasion I wonder if this business of feeding myself and others is really worth so much time and so many words. We might say that eating, fuelling our continued physical existence, is the most banal and the most animalistic of human activities, but all that means is that it is the most fundamental.

We define the ages of our history by which metals were used to make, among other things, cooking pans; for all you might say about art, architecture and philosophy, civilizations come together and develop in order to feed people, to store and move around surplus and to exchange it for hunger, that most fundamental of wants, which we feel from the moment we are born weeping into this world. To have someone assuage this hunger, or to assuage theirs in return... No wonder we are expected to fall in love over dinner, with the shared sense of peace and satisfaction that comes simply from having been well fed, and perhaps from having steadily worked your way through a bottle or two of good or even quite mediocre wine. This is something, I think, that can't be achieved by a single hurried dish, no matter how much time and effort went into it and what histories lie behind the recipe; satisfaction is the province of the meal and comes as much from time well spent as it does from the food itself. When else do you have the chance to sit around a shared table in companiable silence? What else, come to think of it, is a companion but someone with whom you share bread? To cook with someone else, to share expertise and ignorance as you work your way from water to blood, through ingredients and processes and towards eventually a meal, is perhaps even better. In Rachel Roddy's rather wonderful phrase, 'asking someone how they cook something is one way to become friends; showing them how you cook something is another.'

All the cooking is done now, but you may still want to place a large wedge of cheese in the middle of the table and bring back, perhaps, any of the pickles that might have been left from our starter all that time ago, although this return of savoury food is something I find odd after dessert. In France, of course, they have their cheese first, to fill in any corners before the sweet course, which perhaps has something to do with the comparative weight and density of the French dessert and the English pudding. In a bistro in Paris, the cheese course consisted of an entire gold-latticed hostess trolley of cheeses of all kinds – though every one, of course, French – all at the oozing peak of their ripeness, from which you simply made your selection; if this had appeared after the dessert I would probably have eaten a good portion of each along with a fair amount of strong sweet wine, but as it was, knowing I had a course to come, I tried only one or two and perhaps enjoyed it all the more for that. At any rate, I can no longer recall what dessert or even main course I ate in that dark-wooded bistro, but the picture of that groaning cheese trolley and the insouciance with which it was wheeled through the close-packed seats and up to our table is painted indelibly upon my mind; after it and the dessert had come and gone, I expect we had coffee.

There is a theory, expounded in the book *The Devil's Cup*, that coffee, as it replaced beer, cider or wine as the everyday drink of choice for the population of Europe, was largely responsible for the lifting of the fog of superstition and the sudden fashionability of clear, rational thought, which goes by the general name of the Enlightenment. Certainly, if this work is to be believed, everybody prior to that was by today's standards quite drunk most of the time. Rather more sinisterly, Leonardo Sciascia posits the existence of the thick black coffee line, whereby the corruption and criminality of Italy can be measured according to the quality, size and intensity of the espressos, or essentially by proximity to the south. Both of these theories are, I think, more or less fanciful, though it is true that the dense *ristretto* of Sicily is perhaps the finest of all coffee, and certainly of that made in the Italian style.

The Turkish or Greek or Arabic coffee has its points, not least that your fortune can be read in the upturned grounds, but it is one of those things that however carefully you source and construct your ingredients never tastes quite the same as it did at that little café by the beach near Corinth, that table on the hot dusty streets of Kadikoy, or even that diner in the bustle of Cairo; like a dinner of fried fish and too-cold white wine overlooking the harbour, it does not travel well.

Some people only drink Americanos or cappuccinos, which baffles me. A clean cup of coffee from a filter machine or from a French press is good, of course, especially as a mid-morning drink, but after a meal you really need the bitter full stop of an espresso, which acts towards your wine or beer in much the same way that dessert does towards the savoury portion of the meal; not that the coffee counteracts the alcohol, rather it puts an end to it, offering the palate something sufficiently rich and different that you don't really want any more unless, of course, you want a digestif as well. I often do – a Branca Menta, for preference – but only at dinnertime, when it seems perfectly possible that the whole thing could begin again and continue late into the night. No, the pleasure of lunch, I think, is that it is finite, and while to linger over coffee is a fine and civilized thing, none of your guests are likely to sit calling for pot after pot, growing ever more jittery and agitated as you break out first the finest of your single-origin beans, then your standard breakfast blend, and finally, in an attempt to make them leave, that jar of instant decaf, which for some reason always lurks in the back of the cupboard behind the moka, the aeropress, the napoletana, the two cezve and the three cafetieres.

Let us agree then, once and for all, that this meal we have cooked together was lunch, the kind of end-of-winter lunch you have with five good friends, constructed out of the best things of the growing new spring to stave off the cold and the gloom and ultimately to extend life a little longer, to create something, in the twin faces of decay and of death, that might last a few hours or years, if only as a contented memory. It was, I hope, an excellent lunch, but now it is over – and someone has to do the washing up.

23

ON A FINAL PINCH OF SALT

One reason, it seems to me, that the pursuit of perfection in cooking is mistaken is that so much of its enjoyment is completely out of our hands. There are, of course, countless reasons, quite apart from the food, why a meal might be enjoyed or merely endured – the company, the temperature, the holiday feeling, the lighting, the music, even the size and the shape of your plates and cutlery – but setting those aside, it is more likely than not that the meal your diners eat is not, in fact, the one you cooked. Our sense of taste or rather of flavour is such a complex thing, made up not just of the sensations on the tongue but of odour, texture and of course the silent work of memory, which may delight in a smell half-remembered from a happy childhood but balk at one that seems somehow imprinted on pain, the vague recollection of a meal eaten through heavy tears. Even those six basic tastes are perceived differently, not just by different people, who may have more or less actual tastebuds as well as more or less practice at using them, but by the same people at different times; cycles of hormones, mood and illness can all quite noticeably affect our sense of taste, especially of bitterness. Behind the somewhat mystic art of wine-matching lies the very simple principle that what we drink affects the taste of what we eat and vice versa, and a bad match made by a waiter, or by a customer who insists on drinking only heavy reds or indeed dry Martinis throughout his lunch, can ruin the most finely constructed of meals.

Simpler than all of this though, there is the final seasoning, done at the table and entirely under the control of the eater. The more upmarket or at least the more confident sort of restaurant does not allow you to do this, or at least not easily. This is, I think, misguided, though I can appreciate the reasoning behind it. A good cook will do all the seasoning they think necessary themselves, not just with salt but with all the elements and tastes at their disposal, and it is a painful thing to watch someone who, without even tasting their food, scatters salt over a piece of meat that has been brined overnight, knowing that it will be disgusting; as I said before, proper seasoning is very often extreme seasoning, and if as much salt has been added as you think the dish could possibly take then it makes sense not to give people access to any more. You don't, after all, allow them to adjust every aspect of taste themselves, or to come into the kitchen and tell you how to cook. This only works, however, if it is going to be followed through every time, and I have had too many meals, sometimes quite expensive ones, which were simply under-powered, where you could taste, as it were, the ghosts of flavours on the edge of your tongue, but to simply get hold of a little pot of salt seemed close to impossible, at least not without risking the ire of the kitchen and the contempt of our waiter.

At the other end of the scale, at least in price, some cafés, diners and the like will allow you control over almost every distinct taste. You could, I've often thought, accurately rank the supposed quality of an eatery by how much control they give you over your food, from a build-your-own breakfast with eggs to your liking at a greasy spoon, to the zero-choice tasting menus you find at the restaurants recognized by the Michelin Guide, which allow at most for allergies or religion. In a good kebab shop, for example, the kind that perhaps even opens at lunchtime, you are allowed access not just to salt and pepper, which will probably be flakes of dried red capsicums rather than the unrelated black or white spice used as a seasoning in much of Europe, but to olive oil, lemon juice and to sweet pickled chillies, and therefore are able to control, bite by bite, almost the full spectrum of tastes. As with the ketchup, brown sauce, mustard, vinegar, salt and powdery white pepper you can add to that fry-up, or the chilli flakes, oregano, oil, balsamic vinegar and pre-grated Italian hard cheese on the table of a pizzeria, you could argue that this is because of a lack of depth or perhaps delicacy in the food itself; be that as it may, the cooks in such places must realize that theirs is not the final word on the matter of lunch, with the conversation between ingredients continuing onto the table and beyond.

There are people, I know, who consider cooking, at least at the level of so-called fine dining, to be an art form, and speak with the appropriate language of its movements and its meaning. I know that I will never approach this level, either of cooking or of eating, but for myself, I would rather be a craftsman than an artist, and cook what I cook not towards some imagined future posterity but rather out of a concrete present, of life made tangible in water, in vegetable and in blood. Even this might seem a little too much for something as banal as the production and consumption of food to carry. When it comes down to it though, lunch is only food, and whatever else you do to it is almost bound to satisfy or at least fill; if it doesn't, there is always dinner and then breakfast and then the entire parade can begin again, the whole thing taken, along with these and perhaps in the end all words about it, with a good, multifingered pinch of coarse sea salt. This might be obvious to the short-order cook slinging hash in a diner, or to the grill cook carving off pieces of dense, fatty lamb from a rotating spit, but it should be remembered by anyone who ever picks up a knife and an onion and wonders what on earth to do next. What is the point of searching for an impossible perfection when it rests not in the ingredients, which will change from day to day with the seasons and with the weather, and certainly not in the recipe, which is only a more or less inaccurate account of the various things that have been done before, but rather in isolated moments in the mouth and the mind of the eater, where a forkful comes together with a sip and a word to produce something beautiful, that in a second will exist only as a memory and before too long will be gone forever?

ACKNOWLEDGEMENTS

Thank you to
FEDERICA
SARAH
SUSANNAH
AURELIA
MAEVE
OLIA

and to everyone I have ever cooked or eaten with
who all made this book.